7|27

LIFE IN
DARK AGES

a memoir

Other biographies by Ernst Pawel:

The Nightmare of Reason: A Life of Franz Kafka
The Labyrinth of Exile: A Life of Theodor Herzl
The Poet Dying: Heinrich Heine's Last Years

LIFE IN
DARK AGES

a memoir

Ernst Pawel

FROMM INTERNATIONAL
PUBLISHING CORPORATION
NEW YORK

Printed in the United States of America

First U.S. edition

printed on acid-free, recylced paper

Library of Congress Cataloging-in Publication Data
Pawel, Ernst.
    Life in dark ages : a memoir / by Ernst Pawel. — 1st U.S. ed.
      p. cm.
    Includes index.
    ISBN 0-88064-168-1 (alk. paper)
    1. Pawel, Ernst—Biography.   2. Critics—Germany—Biography.
  3. Biographers—United States—Biography.   4. Translators—United States—Biography.   I. Title.
    PT 67.P39A3   1995
    830.9—dc20   94-43605
  [B]   CIP

ONE

There is a hard-edged rage that grips you as you look beyond the precipice into the abyss—rage at having to die in the midst of life, rage at those who will survive you, rage at yourself for having weakened so soon.

So soon—at 72?

Reason has nothing to do with the case, and rage is a perfectly appropriate response, vastly preferable to fear, less painful, less demoralizing. And bearing must be preserved, at all costs. Not because of what others think of you but because of what you want to think of yourself as you go out. Vanity unto death itself, but it has its uses. Panic only amplifies the effect of the blow.

Also, there are the others, the ones who will have to live with your death. Could you live with theirs? I doubt it. I much prefer being remembered to remembering.

So you accept your death? As though you had a choice.

In any case, it is foolish trying to justify one's feelings. *La rai-*

son n'y est pour rien. Still, it is worth recalling that for the past half century I've felt like a survivor, spared while so many of those around me perished—the unlucky ones slaughtered like cattle, the lucky ones killed fighting for a dream. At least they died without learning how futile that fight turned out to be in the end.

I was about to say that the uncertainty is what kills you, but that would be a rather inappropriate hyperbole. What will kill me is not uncertainty, although the tests and decisions can be nerve-wracking even if the ultimate outcome is unlikely to be affected by any of them. I am going to die, but I want to die at the end of life rather than spend the remainder of my days anticipating and mourning my death. For that reason I am determined to resist any heroic measures or procedures with dubious promises of a few added months of survival but which would infringe upon life as I am still able to live and enjoy it. (*Quality of life* is one of those detestable free-market phrases, appropriate to a society where life, like all else, has become a commodity.)

Assuming we know when life ends—when does it begin?

A particularly timely question on a day when the Supreme Court both upheld and gutted *Roe v. Wade*, though neither theology nor the law seem of any particular relevance, because whatever the legal, philosophical or medical evidence, people start living, i.e. become conscious of being alive, neither in utero nor at birth but at widely differing points in their lives.

It took me fourteen years.

Unfair. I did have a childhood, the sort of childhood that passed for normal in the German-Jewish bourgeoisie and in the fabled Berlin of the 1920s, of whose post hoc mythology I remained blissfully ignorant; the Berlin I remembered was grim

and gray, like its people. A concrete desert seething with violence that erupted nightly in its streets, battles between right
and left frowned upon by the sober citizenry because littering
was *verboten* and corpses in the gutter left a mess that
offended the Prussian sense of order. The crematoria later
solved *that* problem.

No cause for complaint. I had a dull, sheltered childhood,
like most of my contemporaries. Our parents led dull, sheltered
lives, though I think they seemed glamorous to us, and would
have been perfectly happy to go on leading dull, sheltered lives
rather than being run over by history and condemned to live in
interesting times.

School put an end to childhood.

The theory and practice of compulsory education, with the
stress on compulsion, constitutes Prussia's most original contribution to the miseries of growing up. First promulgated in 1763
by Frederick II, it retained much of the spirit of the Alte Fritz,
that enlightened homosexual autocrat who befriended Voltaire,
composed flute concerti and loved to make war rather than
love, encouraging his soldiers to give their all for king and
country by goading them with cries of "Do you want to live forever, you sons of bitches?" Hard to beat as a morale booster, but
apparently it worked, just as his compulsory education did, up
to a point and for much the same reason that dog training
does—discipline they call it, although obedience is what the
young ones have beaten into them and the old ones regurgitate
till their brains fall out. Obedience, the blinder the better, has
always been Prussia's pride, sustenance and not-so-secret
weapon. It makes for a land where young and old do what
they're told to do, think what they are told to think, and where
the trains run on time. Always. Even when all else already lay in
ruins, the trains to Auschwitz still ran on time. Do you want to
live forever, you sons of bitches?

So much for my fond memories of childhood. Be it said that I got along reasonably well with my parents, that I was a good student and had no particular problems, personal or otherwise. But I did not really come to life until we moved to Belgrade. *Moved* is hardly *le mot juste*. Fled.

Tomorrow the oncologist. A sophisticated death sentence pronounced on the basis of incriminating medical wizardry.

How did we wash up in Belgrade, of all places, in the spring of '34?

I am not altogether sure. I was barely fourteen years old, an only child, and though my parents prided themselves on progressive ideas and were, in fact, remarkably unauthoritarian in practice, there were certain topics which people of their background and generation simply did not discuss with children. Still, with hindsight I think I can pretty well reconstruct a decision that seemed mildly insane at the time and which probably saved our lives.

Most generalizations about German Jews are bound to be fatuous; which, however, has never discouraged their proliferation. Though a relatively small minority—about 400,000, roughly .6 percent of the total population—they were a heterogeneous lot, ranging from desperately poor to obscenely rich, from left-wing radical to protofascist, from atheist to ultra-Orthodox, and from German patriot to Jewish nationalist, with the preponderance clustered somewhere in the liberal spectrum between these extremes. But by the end of 1932 the virulence and uncompromising racist bent of resurgent anti-Semitism had shattered many illusions; assimilation was a manifest failure, and even the age-old dodge of baptism no longer offered a way out.

Illusions die hard; many a Jewish war veteran duly reported for deportation and death with a row of medals on his chest.

But a good many others took up the challenge; accused of being Jewish, they decided to live up to the charge. This, presumably, is what prompted my parents' seemingly outlandish decision to celebrate my bar mitzvah as I approached my thirteenth birthday.

It took place on Saturday, January 28, 1933. Two days later Adolf Hitler became Chancellor of the German Reich. *Tomorrow the world* . . .

The new Dark Ages were ushered in by fire:

On January 30, a torchlight parade through the streets of Berlin to celebrate Hitler's victory, with frenzied crowds hailing the jackbooted barbarians.

A month later, on February 27, the *Reichstag*—the parliament building—going up in flames, put to the torch by the Nazis so as to legitimize a state of emergency and the arrest of thousands of their opponents on charges of arson and insurrection.

And finally, on May 11, the bonfire of the books, symbolic *Auftakt* to the burning of their authors.

And yet most Jews, serene in their trust in German *Kultur*, sought comfort in shopworn clichés. Economic realities and pressure from abroad, so their mantra went, would soon force Hitler to moderate his views and curb the extremists in his own party. A rational view which, however, turned out to be both dead wrong and deadly. The Nazis were not rational, sense and reason were not part of their creed, and Hitler meant exactly what he had said all along and was determined to carry it out.

Taking him at his word meant leaving the country as soon as possible, yet even those eager to do so found themselves trapped not just by sentiment or sentimentality—a profound attachment to the language, landscape and culture of a land where most had lived for generations—but by formidable constraints of a much more practical nature. In a time of world-wide depression and mass unemployment, penniless foreigners, Jews in particular, were decidedly unwelcome everywhere; the few countries grudgingly willing to admit a limited number of refugees imposed and enforced tough regulations that made it all but impossible for them to earn a living.

Under the circumstances, my parents' decision in the summer of 1933 to abandon what in those initial stages of the Nazi terror still amounted to a comfortable middle-class existence in Berlin and seek refuge in a Balkan capital of more than dubious repute seems little short of heroic in retrospect, quite out of character with my teenage view of them as hopelessly bourgeois and teetering on the brink of senility. They were, in fact, barely into their early forties at the time, and the rest of the picture, I suspect, was equally out of focus. But few children ever get to see their parents with dispassionate objectivity. Which, for all I know, may be just as well.

I would like to think that it was foresight, intuition and principles that motivated their precipitous flight, though I suspect that what mainly shaped their decision was the chaos, ignorance and confusion of the times rather than any discernible logic or rational planning. But it is also true that a leap into the void takes more guts than a careful descent down a firmly planted ladder.

The oncologist turned out to be refreshingly human, competent, related, and he laid out the options without pulling punches but leaving ample room for modest hope. Interesting how people conveying the same message—or the same judgment—can nonetheless leave you with entirely different impressions.

I continue to feel remarkably detached—no doubt a certain depersonalization is bound to take place in all such situations, and the fact that my blood pressure was up even though I felt perfectly calm and relaxed hints at deeper emotions with which I fail or refuse to communicate. Is that bad?

The laws of men can be subverted. No one escapes the laws of nature. Of which death is the most basic one.

Tomorrow the surgeon.

Death sentence confirmed, with thorough, dispassionate and yet decently empathetic explanations. Broncho-alveolar carcinoma, probably multifocal. The tiny spot on the right lung is, in his expert opinion, almost certainly malignant, in which case there is no point in operating on the left one. He proposes a biopsy by direct intervention—a relatively minor procedure, according to him, small scar, though still requiring general anesthesia. If, by a miracle, it should turn out to be negative, there is still time to proceed with the resection on the right side. Otherwise . . .

Otherwise. If I had only myself to worry about, I'd forget about the otherwise and let nature take its course. But as it happens, I am not the main victim in this de-dramatized drama, and I can certainly not afford to voluntarily forgo a chance to extend life. If life it be.

I wonder about this unearned serenity of mine; is it genuine? I had always believed that the one positive aspect of a strong religious faith was this serenity in the face of death, the surrender to god's will and the certainty of an afterlife in paradise or a reasonable facsimile thereof. Whereas I now feel no need whatsoever to avoid reality as I see it. It is as if, having like most humans been afraid of death all my life, now that I have come face to face with it and am constrained to acknowledge it not as a distant inevitability but as an imminent prospect, I no longer have any reason to be afraid.

Pain, suffering, torture may change all that. Will I have the courage to take charge of my own death if it becomes necessary?

• • •

The first shock was the arrival at the railroad station. Spring 1934, a radiant morning after a long night's journey from Budapest, and the Belgrade station a cross between a lunatic asylum and an Oriental bazaar—hordes of peasants, cattle on the tracks, hoarse-voiced Albanian porters lugging huge loads, Gypsy beggars with their own or somebody else's dark-eyed, hauntingly beautiful children waylaying us on the platform while swarms of pickpockets zero in like sharks and two-men patrols of rifle-toting gendarmes represent the shabby, sadly shopworn majesty of the law. Welcome to the Balkans. For my parents, the beginning of heartbreak and exile. For me, the beginning of life.

Probably an exaggeration, a creative reinterpretation rather than a factual recollection of that initial moment, though memory is creative even at its most factual. But the contrast between the drab, orderly, well-run Berlin railroad station we had left two days earlier and the total chaos in which we found ourselves on descending at the other end was real enough. I remember—a factual rather than creative recollection—my mother pathetically trying to keep track of the eight suitcases that contained all our worldly goods while my father struggled to communicate in sign language with what looked like an Albanian bandit chieftain. In the end two of the bandits deftly and almost lovingly lugged all our trunks out to a cab that took us to the Hotel Royal, and when my father offered them what seemed like a barely appropriate tip, they almost kissed his feet. Welcome to the Balkans of prehistory.

Another bronchoscopy, this one decidedly unpleasant, done by a new resident who seemed to think he was dealing with a stuffed toilet. Just to make matters more interesting, the power went off on the machine right in the middle of the procedure, and it took ten minutes for them to get a new one while I lay there with a hose stuck in my trachea and the Valium dripping into my veins. By that time the original one had cooled off sufficiently for the relay to cut back in.

This pose of nonchalant bravado in the face of death is probably just that—a pose. There has to be fear somewhere underneath it, and perhaps I'd be better off getting in touch with it. But I rather doubt if it would improve my mood or my chances, and in any case, I don't feel panicky. I certainly don't want to die, but I cannot conceive of nonbeing, hence cannot conceive of it as a particular menace.

If only I could be spared these constant confrontations with the experts. Battling cancer. How do you battle cancer? Better dying through chemistry?

Belgrade's Hotel Royal was an oasis in the desert of time. The urbane, multilingual concierge and the cut-glass chandeliers in the dining room conveyed illusions of faded glory, but the musty smell, the moth-eaten carpets and the drab décor of the rooms made it abundantly clear that the place had never been more than a third-rate flophouse patronized by cattle dealers, prostitutes and salesmen; if anything, the flock of defrocked German-Jewish professionals who started nesting here in the fall of 1933 in flight from the Nazis raised the tone of the establishment, much to the satisfaction of the concierge, who aside from being a pimp and police spy had also, by the time we got there, advanced to resident bagman and bribe collector for various local rackets. But the hotel was relatively cheap, reasonably clean, with a dingy interior courtyard billed as a garden that satisfied the needs of these particular guests who, though compulsively addicted to fresh air, were reluctant to venture out among the barbarians beyond the walls. Demoralized, disoriented, they sat out there for days on end, rechewing the past, fantasizing about the future and ignoring the present. Their principal occupations were bridge, gossip, and adultery, all of them indulged in with the same world-weary listlessness.

It was an incestuously self-contained universe with no room for children, least of all children who had just barely left childhood behind them and were seething with hormones, illusions and ideals. Oppressive, suffocating, yet at the same time lubriciously intriguing, a sort of respectable whorehouse reeking of smugness and fornication. The fact that I suddenly found myself sleeping on a couch in a hotel room I shared with my parents may have stirred up Oedipal urges, though the unconscious turmoil did not, so far as I know, trouble me any more than did the loss of a room of my own. That my parents, on the other hand, must have been bleeding badly is something I can only appreciate in retrospect; to their credit, they never complained while wrestling with demons of their own. Having to move from a spacious modern apartment into a single bleak room was bad enough, but they had also been exposed to Freudian teachings and were no doubt greatly concerned about the impact of this forced intimacy on the still unformed psyche of their offspring.

Who, hormones raging, proceeded to fall wildly in love with the eighteen-year-old daughter of a Berlin dermatologist and his enigmatic clotheshorse of a wife. Lorna had a pretty face, a provocative ass and a sweet disposition; that she was not overly bright seemed merely one more asset in that it promised to facilitate my salacious intentions. I was well versed in the theory of seduction, having read extensively on the subject, but my practical experience was nonexistent, and since I had no idea how to go about making the first move, I fantasized instead about having her seduce me. Somehow she failed to read my mind, or perhaps she read it only far too accurately for comfort. At any rate, she insisted on treating me like a little brother, and our romance never progressed beyond a few sisterly pecks on the cheek. It ended abruptly when I found out that she regularly slept with older Belgrade businessmen picked by her mother in hopes of snaring one of them into at least a pseudo-marriage so as to acquire a Yugoslav passport and make life easier for the entire family.

I still remember our final heart-to-heart talk, with me feigning a stance of world-weary cynic while all the time the priggish little socialist Boy Scout in me was deeply shocked. I knew that sex was meant to be dirty, in a delicious sort of way; that was part of good clean fun. But to imagine Lorna in bed with some greasy creep old enough to be her father struck me as out-and-out disgusting. Which did not, of course, stop me from imagining.

At least, though, she was the one person who had broken out of the cocoon, made contact, so to speak, with the outside world, which was more than any other resident of this fish tank had done in the many months of self-imposed confinement. She had even picked up a few snippets of Serbian, a feat deemed utterly miraculous by these wooden-tongued ex-Teutons who spent their time playing bridge, musical beds, and waiting. Always waiting.

Waiting for what?

A question rarely asked, because the standard answers—war, revolution, a work permit, the end of Hitler, a new lover, a visa to another planet—were hollow affirmations of futility. The harsh reality was that these alienated aliens had no clue as to what they were waiting for, any more than what it was that awaited them.

For me, on the other hand, Belgrade was life—past, present, future.

Waking up in the morning is consistently unpleasant. Waking into rather than from a nightmare.

The need to make decisions inevitably shatters whatever serenity I am able to muster. Proud as I am of being and wanting to be in charge of my own destiny, the temptation, innate and inbred, of indulging your dependency and entrusting your fate to others never quite vanishes—let the pilot fly this damn crate. This damn crate, however, is what is left of my life, and no one else, whatever their technical competence, will treat it with the same care and respect for its essential nature as I do myself.

TWO

Back to when life began—Belgrade, 1934. A village, a fortress and a state of mind.

Perched on a promontory high above the confluence of the Danube and the Sava, defiant outpost of the Balkans facing the hostile Magyar-Teutonic plains of Pannonia, it has since time immemorial provoked the greed and fury of countless conquerors, from Visigoths and Huns to their modern-day descendants. Whether the spirit of the place shaped those who lived in it or simply attracted a special breed may be debatable; not so the savage pride, spontaneous generosity and sheer pigheaded contentiousness of a population that above all else was intensely and outrageously alive. Emerging as I did from the fetid muck of a necropolis full of petrified mummies, the kaleidoscopic chaos of this unkempt Balkan dump masquerading as a nation's capital struck me as a revelation. I was bewitched by the crowds, the colors, the sounds of an utterly alien language, carried away by a naive exhilaration which, however much it owed to teenage romanticism, forced my eyes open to the world. And first impressions do count; they capture truths that later tend to get blurred or lost altogether in the pea soup of nuanced details. To me the White City never quite lost its magic, and none of what I subsequently came to know about its lower and lowest depths could quite efface the memory of my first encounter with it.

Although I had, without as yet quite realizing it, already been run over by the wheels of history, I had no sense at all of the past and its enduring sway. Berlin was a town without dimensions in time. It got its start in the Middle Ages and in a sense never left them, merely spreading like a complacent fungus over the sandy flats of the March of Brandenburg without striking roots, a shallow blight spawning generations of smug, bigmouthed little Berliners all but indistinguishable from one another. Misfits and outcasts abounded on the margins, there as everywhere, but the broad masses conformed to the norms of tribal conduct and appearance. With pride, be it said. *Ich bin ein Berliner* . . .

As to what passed for history in German schools, it was an indigestible brew of patriotic pap and mnemonics for morons. We learned to rattle off the dynastic succession of the Hohenzollerns and the dates of every battle in the Punic wars, but our only direct exposure to tissue of the living past were repeated school trips to *Sans Souci*, a rococo retreat Frederick the Great had built himself in nearby Potsdam which left right-thinking Prussians slobbering with reverence, even though theirs was clearly a flawed and ambiguous hero who much preferred Frenchmen to Germans and had no use for women at all.

In Belgrade, on the other hand, the roots of human folly ran deep, all the way back into prehistory. Traces of a neolithic settlement had been found, but it was in the fourth century B.C.

that the Illyrians built a fortified settlement on this crest, subsequently destroyed and rebuilt by a succession of conquerors—Romans, Visigoths, Huns, Slavs, Turks, Hungarians, Austrians, Germans—in an ever-mounting spiral of violence that left indelible traces in the geological strata of the city's soul. Those, however, took time to decipher, whereas the physical evidence concentrated in and around the Kalemegdan fortress seemed instantly accessible and, to a teenager's febrile imagination, vastly more interesting.

The highest point directly above the juncture of the two rivers was a sprawling military enclave, a patchwork of structures erected over the course of the last two centuries. It was in 1521 that the Turks conquered Belgrade, and though dislodged time and again by marauding crusaders bent on spreading Christian love by pillage, arson and murder, the wily infidels always managed to sneak back. A Turkish garrison held the fortress until 1867, every so often lobbing a shell into the by then already autonomous Serbian town just to remind the population of Allah's merciful omnipotence.

The fortress, surrounded by crumbling walls topped with barbed wire, was still off limits to civilians, but the rest of the promontory with its deep clefts and fissures had been converted into a park half cultivated, half nature in the raw, much like its creators. Its maze of narrow, deeply shaded footpaths led to a profusion of mysterious ruins—dungeons, graves, archways, towers, walls, mementoes mostly of the Turkish occupation, but some clearly dating back to the Roman presence while others, such as the remnants of an eighteenth-century clock tower, marked the repeated brief but bloody incursions of the Austrians.

The vegetation was lush beyond anything I had ever seen in the parks and woods around Berlin, and it offered a refuge from the brutal heat of early summer that turned the Hotel Royal into a furnace and its inmates into morose bores. Even my own parents were not exempt from the cool, callous contempt that made me wonder why they didn't *do* something about their problems—work permits, money, Hitler, politics, the prospects before us or the lack thereof—instead of pissing away their days yammering and whining.

Typical of the snot-nosed kid I was, buoyed by the glorious and uncompromising arrogance of an age at which one accepts no excuses or ambiguities—why, I refrained from asking, did my father have to keep smoking a pack a day if we were rapidly running out of money?—mindless of the fact that my father and all the other adults were earthquake survivors, stunned and still in a state of shock; their whole world had caved in on them. Or so it seemed at the time. That what they had survived was in fact a mere prelude, initial rumblings, and that most of them would eventually end in unmarked graves when the ground really began to shift under their feet lends a melancholy tinge to this retrospective glimpse of the self-righteous little monster I probably even then half knew myself to be.

One episode, the bitter, rotten tail end of childhood repressed for decades and turned up more or less by accident like a buried bone on a recent visit to the scene of the crime: myself roaming the dusky paths and passageways of the Kalemegdan, spinning intricate, endless daydreams about assassinating Hitler, about massacring Nazis, joining the Yugoslav military and marching back into Berlin at the head of the victorious Serbs while trying to release my unvoiced fear and fury by hurling rocks at the clusters of lizards that all but covered the sun-baked stones of the ancient walls. There were so many of them that even with my rather wayward pitching arm I managed to hit a fair number. And even though I felt sick every time I committed murder, it somehow failed to stop me. I would have had less compunction about killing people, I think, but then, most victims of our darker selves are innocents just seeking a place in the sun. And when, in the dense, jungle-like lower reaches of the park near the Danube I came across an occasional stroller who would eye me with undisguised suspicion, I felt like a serial killer about to be unmasked. I naively assumed these usually massive, middle-aged men to be pedophiles or homosexuals on the prowl. It took some time—and a quick course in the real facts of life—for me to learn that they were plainclothes police looking for clandestine Communist conspirators hiding in the bushes.

Solitude is a gift from heaven, but one not readily appreciated by an active teenager. Never before or since have I been as lonely, as completely cut off from all human contact as during that first Belgrade summer. To those with whom I shared a language I had nothing to say, and beyond the lobby of the Hotel Royal I was deaf and dumb, barely able to decipher the Cyrillic street signs, more inarticulate even than the infants in their carriages. I felt as though I were watching life through a thick, soundproof sheet of glass, unsure whether I was inside looking out or outside looking in.

But what sank in, slowly, was that not only couldn't I communicate with the natives—I no longer had any language I could call my own; my passionate repudiation of Germany and all she stood for also included the very language that had formed my consciousness. And so, a week after my arrival, I began to throw myself into the study of Serbo-Croatian, determined to master the beast within a few months. I did eventually find out that no language will ever truly let itself be mastered, but I also learned enough Serbian to speak it as fluently as a native. And in the meantime the task itself kept me very busy throughout the summer. It also kept me happy. Which, however, had at least as much to do with the teacher as with the subject matter.

Irma S. was a graduate student of German Language and Literature at Belgrade University who lived up the street from the Hotel Royal in an apartment she shared with her parents, two married sisters, their husbands and at least two babies. The family must once have been reasonably affluent, to judge from the profusion of furniture, rugs and knickknacks crammed into every available space; even Irma's chaste cell resembled nothing so much as a storeroom. The father, a shadowy figure forever "on the road," seems to have been an irrepressible optimist convinced that the road would eventually take him back to the prosperity of his early years and restore glamor and purpose to those massive armoires and Louis XIV chairs, but in the meantime the family had fallen on lean times. Even the most upbeat of salesmen could not beat the odds against him in a country where the peasants, eighty percent of the population, were too poor even to afford a box of matches produced by the government monopoly. The sons-in-law, in their late twenties, were university graduates, one a philosopher, the other a historian, two among hundreds, if not thousands, of unemployed young intellectuals spending much of their days in bed and much of their nights in cheap cafés on the outskirts of town plotting to change the world. Like most of their colleagues, they did not even pretend to look for work, pending the revolution. Irma was the only member of the clan to bring in some spare change by giving Serbian lessons. Her fees were ridiculously low, and few pupils lasted more than a few weeks; all they wanted was to be able to haggle in the market and parrot a few phrases. But for some time, as more refugees came drifting in, the turnover was sufficient to keep her in business.

And in the absence of any organized—or even disorganized—efforts on the part of the local Jews to assist us, she became a kind of guardian angel to the refugee colony, supplying information, offering advice, helping with legal formalities and interpreting some of the quainter native customs. It was a role that actually suited her looks and personality far better than that of a teacher; she had the requisite radiance and patience, and her austere, almost intimidating beauty more than made up for her rather marked pedagogical deficiencies. One does not fall in love with an angel. I merely worshipped her, but my devotion did more for my progress in Serbo-Croatian than even the most sophisticated instruction could have accomplished.

Irma set out to teach as she was taught herself—memorizing a set quota of words each day, learning the basic rules of grammar, translating puerile phrases from inane textbooks into elementary German. Being desperately eager to please her, I memorized ten times my assigned daily quota of words, bravely attempted to decode newspaper headlines and public announcements with the aid of the dictionary I carried with me everywhere, and by the end of the first month had acquired enough of a vocabulary to begin on my own initiative to write brief daily compositions in elementary Serbian which, disguised as stylistic exercises, were in fact pathetic efforts to break down her discouraging otherworldly reserve. As an attempt at epistolary seduction the experiment proved a dismal failure; she remained as angelically aloof as ever and gently rebuffed my transparent overtures by limiting her comments exclusively to grammar and syntax rather than content. Yet persistence served a purpose, though not quite the one it was meant to serve: I had accidentally hit upon one of the most efficient methods of acquiring true intimacy with a foreign language. Irma, angel rather than teacher, probably never even noticed.

But it was the guardian angel in her who finally responded, and with quite unexpected vehemence at that, to what I thought was one of my most impersonal and perfunctory essays, the bland account of a radio program.

My parents had befriended a young couple from Frankfurt who had succeeded in transferring a good part of their assets abroad and chose to live in Belgrade because the depressed currency, low cost of living and rock-bottom wages allowed them to wallow in what, by refugee standards, amounted to conspicuous luxury—a large, airy apartment with modern conveniences and live-in help. They owned a powerful shortwave set, and several nights a week we would drop in on them to listen to the German-language broadcasts of Radio Moscow, which offered slanted but often well-informed analyses of German politics and the world situation generally.

For all my fascination with Belgrade and its murky history I had somehow managed to remain completely ignorant of the political realities prevailing in King Alexander's Yugoslavia. Having grown up in the Weimar Republic, I naively assumed that liberal democracy was more or less the rule throughout Europe and that Nazism constituted merely a singular pathological aberration. It was Irma who for the first time, and with an emotional intensity clearly linked to some very personal experiences, enlightened me as to the true nature of this supposedly constitutional monarchy, in actual fact a royal dictatorship in which a cabal of army and police suppressed all dissent by methods which even the Gestapo might have hesitated to copy, at least in those early stages.

After apologizing for her initial outburst and switching to German so as to make sure I understood every word, she proceeded to warn me against ever expressing any sort of sentiment liable to be interpreted as subversive, even in ordinary conversation. "You never know whom you are talking to. Half the people in this town inform on the other half, and if someone denounces you as a Communist, you go to jail and your parents get kicked out of the country."

"Go to jail just for being a Communist?"

"Just for being a Communist. And you don't just go to jail, either," she said, but then stopped herself in time. Another act of grace for which, in retrospect, I owe her gratitude.

She took my composition and methodically tore it into tiny shreds. "Above all, never mention the Soviet Union, in any context."

"One-sixth of the Earth," I protested, parroting Radio Moscow. "They can't just simply make believe it doesn't exist."

"Believe me, they can," she said quietly. "As far as they're concerned, it doesn't exist, and don't you be the one to try and tell them otherwise. The Czar's flag is still flying over the Russian embassy, his ambassador represents a colony of at least a hundred thousand emigrés, and high officials of the Czarist secret police head our own anti-Communist squads. They don't appreciate being reminded of the Soviet Union, and they get particularly upset at any mention of Radio Moscow. I don't mean to scare you, but I would want to be very, very careful."

She did, of course, mean to scare me. And whatever may be said for more progressive methods, scaring people remains one way of teaching them not to set themselves rather than the world on fire.

The old Sunday afternoon blues are back. Ever since I retired ten years ago I was rid of them—for the first time since I started school at age six. Now I can look forward to Mondays busy with phone calls, appointments, interviews, examinations, decisions. Agonizing decisions, as the saying goes, decisions about how to prolong the agony.

Sleep, though, has become a friend. I have pleasant dreams, just as I did twenty-three years ago, when Ruth went into the hospital. Darkness descends when I open my eyes.

The Sunday afternoon blues. Treat them with contempt.

•   •   •

Dr. Anta Khan, a striking Eastern beauty, possibly Turkish, proposes doing a High-Resolution CT scan followed by a needle biopsy. Self-confident and confidence-inspiring, with a brusquely distant yet sympathetic manner. Though of course the procedure in the end is unlikely to resolve much of anything. Still, it is amazing how little it takes to feel good these days—any reprieve gratefully accepted, like a heroin high. Good to the last hour.

The calls from Israel have made me determined to go there in the spring, if I last that long.

The most exciting development that summer was the bloody purge within the Nazi leadership climaxing a long-standing rivalry between Ernst Röhm's brown-shirted storm troopers, Himmler's black-shirted SS, and the various factions of the fast-growing army.

On June 30, 1934, Röhm, a beefy boozehound notorious for his homosexual orgies, was killed by Himmler's henchmen along with several hundred of his top-ranking leaders. At the same time, a number of *Reichswehr* officers with pronounced political ambitions were also eliminated; the official death toll was seventy-five, but the true count—scarcely a matter of great humanitarian concern—has never been established.

It was a cause for great rejoicing among the refugees. Reason played no part in their wishful thinking, and many readily convinced themselves that this bloodbath signaled the end of the Nazi terror. As the oracles at the Hotel Royal would have it, Röhm's storm troopers represented the most plebeian, hence the most radical, element of the Nazi movement; they had to be eliminated as an obstacle to the pursuit of more moderate policies, now that Hitler and his industrialist backers had consolidated their power. At night, hunched over the shortwave set in the Friedlanders' apartment, we listened to Radio Moscow crowing triumphantly about the Nazi purges; their own, still in the early stages, went unmentioned. Even my father, depressed by our increasingly difficult situation, cheered up briefly. "In the long run," he said, "they can't do without the Jews."

He was far from alone in this misconception, but I suppose it helped to keep up his spirits. As for myself, I didn't have the slightest desire ever to go back to Germany. Except that on my rambles in the Kalemegdan the daydreams about war against the Nazis and a victory parade through the Brandenburg Gate grew ever more fanciful and convoluted.

By the end of the summer I had mastered the language sufficiently to carry on a simple conversation. Reading the *Politika* still took much time and effort as I tried to crack the more important articles every morning with the aid of the dictionary, but I no longer felt totally at sea among people speaking Serbian, and much of the time had at least a general idea of what was going on around me.

One result was that the anonymous blur of humanity out in the streets, squares and markets began to assume a focused if complex diversity—Serbs, Hungarians, Albanians, Germans, Russians, Gypsies, Jews. Down by the desolate shore of the Danube I came upon a run-down section of town that had the look and feel of a separate village, in which cats and dogs chased chickens across unpaved streets. Black-clad old women clustered in front of their crumbling one-story houses munching sunflower seeds and chatting away in Ladino, the language of medieval Spain. Though born and raised within this self-contained ghetto, many were barely able to communicate in the language of their native country. Their ancestors, driven out by the Inquisition in 1592, had settled in Belgrade as early as the middle of the seventeenth century, yet while relations between the Sephardic community and their Serbian hosts were marked by a—for their time—quite uncharacteristic tolerance and mutual respect, the women tended to grow up in quasi-Oriental isolation, with no schooling and no outside contacts until the revolutionary upheavals in the wake of the First World War.

Then there was Little Russia, a picture-postcard town within a town where the remnants of Wrangel's defeated army, twenty thousand strong, had settled after the Russian civil war and created a replica of home complete with Russian church, schools, shops and graveyard. King Alexander, educated in St. Petersburg at the court of Nicholas II, remained unswervingly loyal to his imperial patron; the execution by the Bolshevists of the Czar and his family appears to have been a major factor in Alexander's unrelenting hostility to the Soviet Union and his brutal repression of Communists within his own country. In any case, the Kingdom of the South Slavs, cobbled together at Versailles at the end of World War I and later renamed Yugoslavia, welcomed all anti-Bolshevist Russians and made every effort to integrate them by utilizing their professional and administrative skills. It was in no small measure thanks to Russian bureaucrats that the brand-new state succeeded within a matter of months to generate a bureaucracy more Byzantine than some of the oldest and most sophisticated on the continent. And the skills, techniques and personnel of the *Okhrana*, the Czarist secret police, provided the foundation for Belgrade's own Red Squads and their modus operandi.

At the Hotel Royal, the social event of the season was Lorna's marriage to a seventy-seven-year-old Montenegrin gentleman in reduced circumstances who, for considerations unspecified, agreed to confer his name and nationality upon his eighteen-year-old bride. Alas, two days after the wedding the young bride became a widow. It appears that the groom, in spite of his precarious health and lack of practice, was mulishly insistent upon

exercising his conjugal rights and suffered a stroke as a consequence. Everyone seemed to agree that it was a great way to
go, but I wondered; it all depended, after all, on whether what
killed him was ecstasy or frustration. Lorna could presumably
have settled the question, but I didn't have the nerve to ask her.

In a move dictated by mounting despair, my father in the
meantime had gone into partnership with Lorna's father on a
project to manufacture and sell their own brand of toothpaste;
the idea was to make Lorna the president of the corporation,
since the law required that it be headed by a Yugoslav citizen.
This was merely the latest—and, as it turned out, the last—in a
series of quixotic schemes, all of which fizzled long before they
ever got off the ground. Be it said, however, that business acu-
men was generally in short supply among the refugees, and the
few who possessed it tended not to waste their time in the stag-
nant backwaters of somnolent Balkan capitals. The one-room
toothpaste factory with its hand-operated tube-filling and sealing machine lasted almost an entire month, a rather happy one
during which my father perked up noticeably, concocting mix-
tures of various flavors and colors. But by the end of August
operations folded; the two business geniuses discovered that
they had no way of marketing their product; in fact, I'm not
sure they had ever given any serious thought to that aspect of
the business in the first place. On the other hand, I wonder if
there even *was* a market for toothpaste in a land where few
people brushed their teeth and those sissified enough to do so
probably used sand or plain grit.

School began in September, and in order to register I needed
the approval of the Ministry of Education. This, like any transaction with a government office, required a Petition, and no Petition would be considered or even merit so much as a denial
unless it was drawn up according to regulations and in the man-

ner prescribed by law and tradition, i.e., with a calligraphy pen on the left side of a page of special bond paper folded in half and provided with the requisite number of duly canceled tax stamps. Neither neatness nor calligraphy are among my talents, and a day of trying, under Irma's guidance, to meet at least the minimum standards almost resulted in a nervous breakdown for both of us. But in the end I managed to produce something halfway acceptable, took it to the appropriate office and, on payment of yet another tax, was quite literally given the seal of approval: I was to report to the First Boys' High School on Czar Dushan Street on the morning of September 11. A student cap and the appropriate insignia were mandatory.

THREE

The surroundings were not altogether unfamiliar. Form follows function, and the sinister four-story school building on Czar Dushan Street looked like a prison or a military barracks. Built around the turn of the century, in the days before girls went on to high school, it was now made to do double duty, housing both a boys' and a girls' *Gymnasium*, each of which occupied the premises at different times of the day. We used it mornings when I first started, switching to afternoon sessions three months later. Unlike the triage practiced in the German *Kulturstaat*, where academic education beyond the fifth grade became sufficiently expensive to make it a mark of class division, schooling in this backwater of civilization was practically free of charge from first grade all the way through postgraduate studies. As a result, demand even in the 1930s had already begun to outstrip available facilities. Nevertheless, one serendipitous by-product of this time-sharing arrangement was the opportunity for anonymous romance. Students regularly left notes in the desks they shared with unknown partners of the opposite sex, and quite a few of their missives apparently managed to elude the intrusive snooping and malevolent vigilance of the teachers.

Those teachers were the enemy, and the lines were clearly drawn. No prisoners taken, no quarters given, and much of what passed for classroom study was in fact class warfare, pitting wildly inventive future guerrilla fighters against the traditional but no less ruthless forces of the establishment. It took no time to discover that my new classmates had absolutely nothing in common with those snivelling little soldiers-to-be whom I was used to back in Berlin. Communication posed a bit of a problem during the early days; the earthy vernacular they habitually used was not the sort of language taught by the saintly Irma, but they were more than willing to remedy my linguistic deficiencies. Altogether they welcomed the rather awkward and prissy stranger with a generous enthusiasm totally disorienting in the beginning, the more so since I had expected nothing but wary suspicion, the kind of reception a Serbian newcomer to Berlin would have been given by my former classmates. Nothing wary or half-hearted about these kids, a species utterly different from the one I had grown up with; that much I sensed from the moment I walked into the classroom. What took some time to learn was that their uncompromising fervor cut both ways, that they divided the world into friend and foe, and that they could be as ruthless in their hate as they were generous in their love. And that their tender care for me was quite unearned on my part, at least to begin with; as a refugee from Nazism—the first one they had ever met in the flesh—I was simply the beneficiary of their passionate antifascist convictions. With the exception of three stool pigeons known and shunned as such, every student in that class considered himself a fighter in the vanguard of the international proletariat.

They were very young. And most of them died long before they had a chance to grow old.

It was the Gypsy who first took me under his wing.

His real name was Sreten Mitrovich, half Serb, half Montenegrin, he explained, with a deprecatory shrug as though to apologize for the unseemly mention of a fact that should count for nothing among us enlightened internationalists, but that nonetheless clearly mattered to him in ways I was totally unable to grasp at the time. His nickname seemed merely descriptive, but I wonder if his own mirror image—the slim-waisted, sinewy body, swarthy complexion, black hair and flashing black eyes—might not have made him needlessly defensive about his origins. For it was not as though we, principled enemies of any racial bias, had anything against the Gypsy tinkers who roamed the unforgiving hills of Montenegro and were sometimes called upon to substitute for husbands gone to war, to hell, or to America.

He had, at any rate, no cause to be anything but proud of his heritage, being by far the brightest star in a class where chess games without board or figures were commonplace and where teenagers argued about books, politics and Marxist philosophy with a passion reserved elsewhere for soccer and movies. The Gypsy was brilliant in every single subject, superior in most of them to the defrocked clerics and assorted mediocrities posing as teachers, one reason why they seldom gave him a better than passing grade. He could not have cared less. Nor did he fail to let them know it.

And this extraordinary character, out of what I naively assumed to be pure sympathy, did everything possible to ease my way into this strange new world. He helped me with the homework, suitably corrupted my language, and introduced me to his friends; that on occasion he also defended me against stupid nitpicking on the part of the teachers proved less than helpful, but mere expediency never stopped any of these kids from forcefully voicing their opinions. He was a born leader, which is why it took me an unseemly long time to realize that the authority he exercised among not only my classmates but throughout the school also derived from less intangible achievements.

I began to have an inkling of this when told that this barely sixteen-year-old had already been jailed twice for subversive activities, and that during his latest arrest he had withstood a particularly brutal beating without betraying any of his comrades.

Courage, in that unhappy land, is commonplace, a glut on the market. The true mark of manhood—and of womanhood, god knows—is the ability to resist torture. Woe unto the land that needs heroes.

But by the time he asked for my help with the Wilhelm Reich project, about three weeks into our friendship, I could no longer entertain any doubts about the not-so-secret life of my friend and mentor.

High-Resolution CT Scan, the ultimate technological invasion of the body snatchers. My lung looks like a map of the heavens, with a drift of nebulae signaling the ominous presence of death. Strange how one learns to live in the shadow of Thanatos, which yet asserts itself in the wild surge of its life-affirming antagonist, whose enduring power transcends age itself.

I wake up in the morning, take a deep breath, decide that I am still alive, and proceed to seize the day, happy when I can structure it myself and don't have any doctors' appointments. And so, from day to day—and from night to night—as though it, and I, would go on forever.

•   •   •

The Gypsy was a leader of the clandestine Communist organization in the school—too conspicuous, perhaps, to be the supreme wire-puller behind the scenes, but he almost certainly headed the cell in our class and was clearly one of the most promising young party recruits and recruiters. I tried to convince myself that this had nothing to do with me; he was just a friend, I had ample reason to be grateful to him, and his politics were none of my business. But several incidents soon convinced me otherwise.

The first was a unique educational experience, some ten days into the school year, when suddenly in the midst of a very dull Latin class the door was flung open and a squat, porcine young man burst into the classroom, flanked by two rifle-toting policemen. He stepped up to the podium and in a low voice, his pale watery eyes fixed on a spot far above and beyond our range, ordered us to pile all our books on top of our desks and stand at attention in the aisles. He then proceeded very carefully and methodically to examine the piles, opening every single book while the probably illiterate gendarmes checked underneath the desks and in the bags, searching for forbidden fruit among the dead straw of math texts and Latin grammars.

And sure enough, they found some highly explosive block-busters—two copies of Upton Sinclair's *The Jungle*, one of the most popular of subversive classics and constantly circulating in the book-starved underground, along with Jack London's *Iron Heel* and Maxim Gorki's *The Mother*. At the conclusion of the raid the four culprits, one of them snivelling, the others pale but defiant, were arrested and marched out of the room.

"Ten days, most likely," said the Gypsy later that morning. "At least that's the usual dose in a first arrest. They'll beat the shit out of them at police headquarters, lock 'em in the basement with the blood-soaked lumps of flesh just back from torture, then bill the parents for room and board. Reeducation."

"Does it work?"

He shrugged. "Some kids scare more easily than others. But at least we get to tell the cowards from the ones we can count on."

I knew, of course, about Gestapo practices, about torture cellars and Nazi concentration camps, but here for the first time I saw myself confronted with a very personal question, acute and anything but theoretical: How would I behave under torture?

It has, I think, been my—under the circumstances, rare— good fortune never to have had my courage put to the test. I don't believe I could have lived up to the Gypsy's exalted standards.

At the time I fudged the issue as behooves a big-mouthed teenager and put the blame instead on my parents, on our precarious status as barely tolerated refugees. He agreed, or made believe he did, but promptly got me involved in a potentially much more dangerous enterprise.

The needle biopsy under a CT scan turned out to be an exquisitely unpleasant procedure, mostly because I was not permitted to breathe deeply and thus could not induce proper relaxation. In fact, panting like a dog and having to stop breathing every minute or so amounted to deliberate hyperventilation; the aftermath and recovery were equally unpleasant, despite the fact that doctors as well as nurses were exceptionally caring as well as proficient.

I am not eager to die, but I am even less eager to have what remains of my life wrecked by treatments of more than dubious efficacy.

The results of the biopsy will presumably be known by Monday. I don't know what to hope for; either way I lose. Although as it now stands, I think that even should it turn out negative, I won't pursue the matter any further and simply assume that we are dealing here with a multifocal malignancy which rules out surgery.

I have infinitely much to be grateful for, but of all the major and minor miracles that shaped my life, the greatest and most enduring by far is the love story that began over fifty years ago and has not only continued but is reaching a climactic affirmation in this final phase. And the children and their families are very much part of it. What more can one ask of life, by way of fulfillment?

But every red, white or blue-blooded American, a consumer by definition, consuming while being consumed, wants to have and to hold—more, better, bigger, and forever. Don't knock the greedy and the disgruntled; they are what's made this country big. Disgruntled customers should, by rights, be much more ready to die than those of us who feel that we got our share of living and have every reason to want more, but I rather doubt if they do.

The Gypsy lived with his mother and two younger brothers in a tiny three-room apartment that was part of a barrackslike tenement on the outskirts of town, in a desolate section suitably close to the cemetery. His father, he told me, had died of tuberculosis some years earlier, still a fairly common fate at the time in that part of the world. The widow, indomitable though far from healthy herself, had raised the three boys on a minuscule pension with some help from the family. She was a tiny, leather-skinned bag of bones wearing a simple black peasant smock, but she welcomed me to her tidy little realm with the proud airs of a queen receiving a foreign ambassador, and I did my best to live up to the role. The Gypsy himself underwent a strange kind of transformation in her presence, his perpetual sneer yielding briefly to a tenderness just short of maudlin. He obviously worshipped his mother, and in her eyes he in turn could do no wrong. She was a proud woman and a tough one who survived the war against the Nazis, only to go mad after the liberation because there was nothing anymore to keep her busy; none of her three boys came back from the wars, and none had left her even so much as a grave to take care of.

There were many women like her, half a century ago, all throughout that tortured land. The thousands more now in our own time prove that reason has no chance against the seeds of madness that seem to thrive in the bloody soil.

The Gypsy introduced me to her as "a comrade who escaped from the German fascists and is going to help us with some important work," a piece of information that caught me by surprise. But the rites of Serbian hospitality required her to feed me a snack, and she served up the watery cocoa and rock-hard cake with understated ceremony, making conversation and complimenting me on my command of the language while I began to suspect a trap. And a trap it turned out to be, deftly set and sprung.

After the meal the Gypsy and I went for a walk, ending up on a bench in the cemetery where he pulled a book out from under his coat. The cover and title page had been ripped off, for security reasons, as he explained. "Have you ever heard of Wilhelm Reich?" he wanted to know.

In further pursuit of expert opinions, another foray into futility motivated, or at any rate rationalized, by a sense of responsibility: one owes it to oneself and others to explore all possibilities, even though from the very first I had not only been convinced of the inexorable fatality of this judgment but also determined not to submit to any gruesome violations of my physical and emotional integrity just in order to *DO* something for the sake of doing. Memorial Hospital exemplifies that approach, but it also represents hope to the desperate, and in many instances undoubtedly achieves what they call miracles. No miracle was offered me, which speaks in their favor; they were honest enough to admit that surgery was the only remote hope of anything resembling a cure, and urged me to resolve the question of the left lung infiltration one way or another. Much more concise and, in his way, much more humane and sensitive was my son Michael's friend, a seasoned oncologist with intimations of wisdom who laid out the options more clearly—and inevitably more mercilessly—than anyone else, obviously taking his cue from my own attitude and approach. He voiced his own contempt for chemotherapy—thirty-five to fifty percent response rate, meaning a very temporary shrinkage of the tumor regardless of what happens to the patient—but admitted that he administered it if patients insisted. According to him, it made no ultimate difference in the length of survival but involved untold misery, including frequent hospitalizations. The plain substance of what he communicated was that nothing offered any hope—very rough on Ruth, like most of what is happening, much rougher on her than on me somehow, and I don't know how to help her. Fudging things certainly is no help; on the other hand, my own defenses—a brutal confrontation with reality and a deliberate avoidance of all tangential sentimentality— sometimes seem gratuitously cruel. Again—I don't think I could muster her strength if the situation were reversed. Another reason to be grateful.

Wilhelm Reich.

A loose cannon, a bull on the loose, and one of Freud's more promising pupils who, in the late 1920s, tried for a synthesis of psychoanalysis and Marxism for which he was excommunicated by the Master and, during a brief guest tour with the Communist Party, managed to outrage the comrades as quickly as he outraged everyone he ever worked or lived with, which promptly earned him another excommunication, this time from the party. His later fame and notoriety as the prophet of the Orgone box still lay ahead, but during his passing flirtation with the working class he had written a short, lucid and idiosyncratically opinionated sex manual. Condemning the standard practices of masturbation and teenage petting as effete and potentially harmful compromises, *The Sexual Struggle of Youth* called for vigorous all-out screwing among youthful proletarians by way of rebellion against bourgeois mores and capitalist oppression. But while the link between orgasm and liberation clearly foreshadowed Reich's subsequent ideological evolution, the booklet also contained a great deal of sound information and practical advice, both in notoriously short supply. It remained deservedly popular in left-leaning German youth movements, although the Communists almost immediately denounced and banned it along with its author. At any rate, by 1934 the Party in its ex- and in-cathedra infallibility had long since abandoned its early stance in favor of "free love" and embraced the hypocritical puritanism of the Stalinist era.

The Yugoslav comrades, however, were out of touch as well as out of synch with the Kremlin, and still zigged when the party line called for zagging. The absence of any diplomatic links or trade relations with the Soviet Union as well as the brutal repression of domestic Communism greatly complicated communications between Moscow and its local sympathizers. Even the nominal Stalin-approved national leadership operated out of Vienna, a rare stroke of good fortune for Yugoslavia's underground party, which was thus forced to develop its own grassroots leaders on the spot; both the successful Partisan resistance in World War II as well as the postwar break with Stalin undoubtedly owed much to those years of isolation and the resultant traditions of relative independence.

Thus it came about that the Gypsy and his flock still

preached and practiced free love; it was not, in fact, till the outbreak of the war that they went puritanical with a vengeance. It required no great powers of persuasion on his part to convince me of the theoretical merits of uninhibited sex; he was preaching to the converted. But instead of offering some practical assistance in the pursuit of this laudable goal, he explained that they—whoever "they" were—had been struggling for months to translate Reich's manual and been utterly befuddled and frustrated by their skimpy high-school German. Would I be willing to help out?

At a time when terminal illness itself was still a morbid fantasy to play with—not, of course, altogether beyond the realm of possibility but essentially an exercise in existential options with no real personal relevance—I used to think of it as a state of invulnerability that would free me from any constraints of law or convention. I would be free to do whatever I wanted, commit any outrage, any crime without fear of punishment, kill some of those bastards—Sharon, Shamir, Kahane, the leaders of the Chetnik irregulars, German neo-Nazis, LePen—I'd always wanted to do away with and go out in a blaze of inglorious glory.

Now that this particular fantasy has become a nightmare come true, the charm has gone out of it. There is simply no way I can make a difference by killing people. There is simply no way I can make a difference in a world gone wholly and perhaps irremediably insane. Which should make leaving it that much easier.

And so, instead, I write. Why?

Because writing is what a writer does, compulsively, to the end. An effort to understand, or at least to try and explain to ourselves what is going on. Futile, of course, as futile as trying to improve the world by wholesale assassinations, not merely

because understanding is beyond us but because there probably is nothing there to understand. God may not play dice, but
whatever it does play, it makes up the rules as it goes along.

Another consultation with the surgeon and, as expected,
confusion compounded. He seems to think that he could par-
tially resect the left lung, with no serious impact on my life and
a good chance of at least arresting the cancer, *providing* the
spot on the right side turns out to be nonmalignant on a direct
open lung biopsy. A very long chance, but can I afford not to
take it?

I dread the thought of again spending time in the hospital,
the whole rigmarole of tests, surgery, recovery. Having more or
less come to terms with the idea of doing nothing, of just letting nature—or death—take its course, I found myself almost
disappointed at being told that the inevitable was not necessarily so, that the left side was treatable, and that despite the high
probability of malignancy on the right side nothing could nor
should be taken for granted without a definite confirmation one
way or another.

Which once again calls for grace under pressure. Heming-
way, sad old faker who never grew up, came up with the ideal
recipe for faking courage.

FOUR

The Gypsy had recruited two of his comrades, both supposedly familiar with German; Otto's Viennese parents and Betty's family name—Birnbaum, "pear tree"—plus a guttural Teutonic *r* apparently sufficed to qualify them as ad hoc linguists, although the Gypsy and those whose orders he was carrying out may simply not have had much of a choice.

For about a month the four of us met two or three afternoons a week, always in a different place, careful never to arrive or leave at the same time "so as not to arouse suspicion." The rituals of conspiracy, which the Gypsy enforced with uncompromising rigor, seemed childish at first, but in due course I learned to appreciate the vital importance of these games. There are times when paranoia is the most rational strategy for survival.

The three dozen or so pages of the Reich book the Gypsy's comrades had attempted to translate were a disaster; the bits of German they had picked up at home simply did not give them enough of a grounding even to use the dictionary with discretion. Novices all, we wasted the first few meetings trying to fix the most egregious blunders until it became clear that the only efficient way to proceed was to start all over again. We learned fast. I translated the German text into clumsy but literal Serbian, which the three of them collectively corrected and refined. Betty, who had access to a typewriter at home, took down the final version in her diminutive, almost microscopic handwriting and brought the typed pages to the next meeting, where the Gypsy took charge of them. Those wild sessions taught me more about both Serbian and German than I could ever have learned in a more formal setting, but Reich's message of sexual revolution seemed to have a curiously anti-erotic effect on all of us. He took the fun out of our still tentative and hesitant first fumblings by denouncing them as unhealthy—or bourgeois, which amounted to the same—and, with didactic pedantry, insisted on full-fledged intercourse as the only road to both individual fulfillment and collective bliss. He provided helpful household hints: diagrams of the sex organs that could make a Casanova go limp, and information about birth control and venereal diseases along with basic instruction on the techniques of coitus. I suppose we were *entre deux âges*, desperately wanting sex and just as desperately scared of it; all I know is that however valuable Reich's advice may have proved to the uninformed proletarian masses, it queered my relationship with Betty and in fact complicated my budding sex life for some time thereafter.

Seated on the living-room couch, immaculately dressed, from top hat to black patent leather shoes, a ghastly smirk on his powder-white face, he sardonically congratulates me for having obtained a temporary stay of execution.

Can anyone ever hope for more?

Cinematic cliché overpowering self-generated fantasy, which experiences death as a slow, cunning invader, parasitical resident of our very own flesh and blood from the day we are born.

The open lung biopsy revealed, against all the odds, that the infiltration in the right lung was benign after all, scar tissue that may have been there since childhood. A stunning piece of news—stunning even to the surgeon—that necessitates a complete reorientation, away from the resigned acceptance of death toward an affirmation of life—a surprisingly difficult step, rendered all the harder since the prospect of extensive surgery on the left lung scared me more than I was willing to admit to myself. But Ruth's reaction and that of the children was enough to make it all worthwhile.

The surgery itself took place at two distinct levels, smooth on the surface, with no technical hitches and a remarkably easy and painless forty-eight-hour aftermath thanks to the epidural analgesia, and yet something must have got stirred up deep inside. Part of it may have been a medication-induced nausea and anorexia, but it merely reinforced a growing paranoia in which the hospital, for all the care and genuine concern on the part of the staff and the relative comfort of the arrangements, began to assume the dimensions of a nightmare and imposed visions of Auschwitz and the Gulag. I suspect that the physical trauma combined with normal anxiety roiled some of the deeper layers of panic that I had learned if not to master then at least to plaster over with a dense concoction of rhetoric, self-deception and pseudowisdom.

Two weeks into convalescence I find it difficult to reconcile myself to the extreme weakness, the slow progress, the multiplicity of handicaps—pulmonary, coronary, arthritic. Having been given a chance at life, I have become increasingly hypochondriacal about things which, in the face of imminent death,

seemed relatively trivial. There is, above all, the wistful realization that a return to "normal" will not mean a return to the
state of benign innocence and physical prodigality of younger
years and that I will grow increasingly conscious of my limita-
tions. The challenge will be to maintain a measure of spiritual
and intellectual vigor, *malgré tout*.

The obsessive return, day and night, to the diagnosis,
surgery, the hospital, the aftermath, and the extreme difficulty
of focusing on the future, the task ahead. Pain and weakness
make it that much harder to exorcise or at least rein in the morbid thoughts and to deal with a strange emotional anesthesia, a
flatness of feeling that in some weird way corresponds to the
sense of armor-plated constriction in my chest.

Toward an affirmation of life . . .

October 9, 1934.

Radio was still in its primitive stages, few households in Belgrade possessed a set, and yet communication was instanta-
neous; rumors spread with the speed of light rather than
sound. King Alexander I of Yugoslavia, it was said, had been
assassinated by a Croatian terrorist in Marseille.

Hours later special editions confirmed the fact and added a
few confused and confusing details. The king, on a good will
mission to France, had disembarked at Marseille where, welcomed by French foreign minister Louis Barthou, he had been
driven in an open car from the dock to the city center. The terrorist had leapt onto the running board and shot both the king
and Barthou before being himself slashed to death by the
antique sabres of the mounted military escort.

I am sure there were many Serbs who were heartbroken and
who mourned in Alexander Karageorgevich their king and
tribal chieftain, but none of my newfound friends and comrades

shed any tears and their view of him as a red-baiting tyrant, though oversimplified and scarcely objective, was probably closer to the truth than the official eulogy of the popular democrat martyred in the cause of peace and South Slav unity.

And yet:

Whether grief-stricken or secretly elated, almost everyone felt a deep sense of foreboding. An unnatural quiet descended upon Belgrade that afternoon and evening. The cafés were closed, soldiers patrolled the streets, there was talk of war in the air, and in the lobby of the Hotel Royal my demoralized, chain-smoking fellow refugees speculated about what would happen to them in the event of actual hostilities. I must confess that I found the prospect of coeducational internment in a prisoner-of-war camp enormously exciting; my hormone-driven teenage imagination pictured a sort of vacation colony for grown-ups, with unlimited opportunities for putting Willy Reich's how-to manual to practical use.

How green were our dreams.

In the course of the evening, shortwave reports from Prague, Vienna and Moscow gave details of the assassination, whose sinister implications we were simply too ignorant and too innocent to appreciate at the time. The murderer was said to have been a Macedonian terrorist trained in a paramilitary camp run by the separatist Croatian Ustashi at Yanka Puzsta, on the Hungarian side of the border, under the not-so-secret auspices of the Italian fascists. It was a blatant attempt to further destabilize the already more than shaky union of South Slavs, with Rome and Berlin ready to pounce and devour the pieces.

It could have worked.

There were Serbs ready to go to war. There were always Serbs ready to go to war—"lest they might have to go to work instead," my poet friend Trifunovich sneered when I once told him the story, but that was years later, and he, a Serb himself,

not an unbiased observer. Ready to take on the whole damn
world, they were, if need be, heedless of consequences, as
indifferent to the odds as to death itself.

It was on that occasion that for the first time I heard of the
Chetniks. The original Chetniks had been legendary Montenegrin guerrilla fighters against the Turks. Their latter-day reincarnation, however, was a semiclandestine paramilitary organization bent on righting five hundred years of wrongs done the
Serbs by god, history, Muslims, Catholics, Communists and Austrians, but above all by the treacherous Papist Croats, cunning
flunkies of the Habsburg oppressors.

Back in 1934, however, caution and wily politicians prevailed one more time over the bearded fanatics who strutted
about like drunken peacocks in their black uniforms and
crossed bandoleers. Alexander was declared a martyr in the
cause of unity, his dying words reported to have been "Preserve
Yugoslavia." What, if anything, he really said is anybody's guess,
but my classmates came up with some truly imaginative ideas.

They had zero respect for authority, and their seemingly total
lack of reverence for any sort of tradition secular or religious
felt enormously liberating to anyone burning, like myself, with
the spirit of teenage rebellion without any clear notion of what
to rebel against. Years later, coming across some of them in the
ranks of Tito's Partisans, I realized that authority and tradition
had caught up with them in the end and that the anarchic,
nihilistic freedom of thought that had marked their teens had
been a passing phase.

But a glorious one while it lasted, even if some of the manifestations were less than hilarious. On the morning after the
assassination, the entire student body assembled in the school-
yard for a somber memorial meeting. The king was to be eulogized by the principal as well as by several teachers and a

Greek Orthodox priest, and according to my suspiciously exuberant comrades, custom called for everyone to utter a reverent "Glory be unto him" every time the martyred Alexander's name was mentioned. "And make damn sure you say it," the Gypsy warned me. "The rat finks are out full force watching lips. If they catch you not flashing your teeth, you'll be in big, big trouble."

All of which was true, except that instead of the traditional *"Slava mu"* for "Glory be unto him," with which at the time I was not yet familiar, they tried to persuade me that an equally unfamiliar, gross but rather esoteric obscenity was in fact the Church-Slavonic formula which tradition called for under the circumstances. I ended up just moving my lips without making a sound, but they were so enormously pleased with themselves for having tricked me into cursing the king and his assorted relatives that I didn't have the heart to disabuse them.

Still—why this hatred?

"With us, it's either-or. Either you hate, or you love. Him we hated."

Of love there is nothing left, this half century later, and hate has exploded in the snarling rage of drunken goons.

Tito is whom they blame as they cut each other's throats.

A mere fifty years after Auschwitz another holocaust. Sarajevo. Kragujevac. Dubrovnik. Dozens, hundreds of towns, villages, hamlets throughout what used to be Yugoslavia. No coldly efficient German organization here, no trains running on time, and above all no hypocrisy. This is Balkan-style slaughter, death handmade and delivered the old-fashioned way. Person to person. With glee. Killers in love with their work, and good at it.

And just like the last time, no one lifts a finger to stop the butchers or to help the victims.

•　　•　　•

On the day of the official funeral all of Belgrade's schoolchildren were made to line the route of the procession, and as I stood with my class at the curb of Duke Michael Street, I had a front-row view of the funeral cortege. In utter silence, the frozen silence of a nightmare, the coffin on the gun carriage rolled slowly past us, followed by the lone figure of a small child incongruously dressed up in a colonel's uniform and striving with pathetic determination to live up to the new role that had suddenly been thrust upon him. A frail, delicate youngster who had been happily attending public school in Britain, twelve-year-old King Peter II struggled to imitate a measured military stride and posture, head up, eyes straight ahead, but for all his brave efforts the diminutive warrior looked like nothing so much as a frail and befuddled little boy who had just lost his father.

Sniffles, sobs and weeping in the crowd broke the silence as he passed, followed by the horse-drawn carriage bearing his widowed mother and two younger brothers. In their wake came a phalanx of foreign dignitaries trotting along in a single row that stretched across the entire street, and thus it happened that the bemedaled, pig-faced Hermann Goering at the outermost right flank nearly brushed up against me as he passed, close enough for me to have stuck a knife into his belly.

One of many heroic deeds undone but often dreamt about.

Refugees, like other hunted species, scent danger everywhere. And usually for good reason. The death of Alexander spread fear in the dim cubicles of the Hotel Royal.

He had been no humanitarian. Fierce anti-Bolshevism and loyalty to his Czarist patrons had made him grant asylum to thousands of Russian emigrés, but the victims of fascism elicited no such sympathy on his part. Still, he was known to be solidly pro-French, and although Jewish refugees, with the exception of a few specialists, were not allowed to work, their residence permits had thus far been renewed every three months. We knew very little, scandalously little about the people of this country among whom we expected somehow to survive the apocalypse, and nothing at all about the three men appointed to run it until King Peter came of age, except that the regency spelled change and that any change was bound to be for the worse. This not very profound thought required no gift of prophecy but turned out to be true nonetheless.

My Communist buddies, much though they reviled the late king, were equally convinced that things were bound to get considerably worse under the new troika—two sleazy fascist politicians and one notorious playboy prince, a Greek cousin of the Queen Mother. But the prospect of dramatically increased repression, economic disaster and political chaos seemed to cheer them to no end. It would, they thought, prepare the ground for the Leninist seed. The king is dead, long live the revolution.

It was not until some years later that, guided or, more accurately, prodded and provoked by one Miroslav Jovanovich, unsung genius of premodern historiography and author of the greatest unwritten history of Serbia, I began to question some of the simplistic certainties of my Marxist playmates. Miroslav was quite fittingly buried in the ruins of his favorite café on Easter Sunday 1941, when Hitler's *Luftwaffe* all but leveled the city. A self-taught polymath and, like most autodidacts, a cantankerous old bastard much like myself at the present stage in my life, he could be woefully off the mark, but he taught me, by sneers rather than sermons, never to take anything for granted.

"King, my ass," he said, referring to the late martyred monarch. "They were a dynasty of peasants. Pig breeders. And Alexander wasn't even in the line of succession. He screwed his older brother out of his birthright and buried him in prison. What a monster. But what a man."

Followed the Gothic tale of Prince George, the original crown prince, who in 1908 had been forced to abdicate in favor of his younger brother by a conspiracy that accused him of having killed his valet in a fit of rage. Popular opinion was divided among those who accepted the official version of George's insanity and those convinced that the power-mad Alexander had plotted his brother's downfall. In any event, with Alexander's ascent to the throne in 1921 his brother George vanished from the face of the earth, a prisoner and nonperson until freed by the Nazi invaders, of all people, who allowed him to settle in Belgrade, where he lived out his life quietly and modestly as a pensioner of Tito's state.

The late fall boat ride down the Danube to the little town of Smederevo was an annual school tradition. It is usually hard to say how such traditions originate, but in this instance I am reasonably certain that the famous vineyards surrounding a town in which there was a winery in nearly every house had much if not everything to do with it. This, however, I had no way of knowing when we first set out early in the morning. The trip down the river took about two hours, which we mostly spent singing revolutionary songs on the upper deck while the teachers hid in the cabin below, wisely sticking together for safety and comfort; there was a corpus of legends surrounding these annual exercises in brotherly love that included some monumental brawls as well as several very wet teachers fished out of the Danube more dead than alive.

I still remember the sound of those brash young voices roaring spitefully into the wind, and the sense of kinship, of being part of a rebel tribe, but the mood changed abruptly the moment we landed. Within minutes I found myself all alone. Students and teachers alike had scattered, drifting through town in small groups bent on getting their fill of as much free wine as the countless wine-tasting establishments would allow. Apparently they allowed plenty, though it probably didn't take all that much to get these youngsters soused. By the time they came trickling back to the pier, the older ones still braying and howling, most of the younger ones already sick and subdued, they were a pretty sorry lot.

And as, on the return trip, clusters of my comrades lay sprawled out on deck atoning for their sins, the little Prussian prig in me, stone-sober and outraged, steeped in the youth movement doctrine of abstinence from liquor and from cigarettes, had the temerity to lecture them on socialist morality.

I can only assume that they were simply too sick to throw me overboard.

FIVE

I thought of them as children of the light—bursting with untamed energy, wild illusions, an irrepressible sense of humor, good will, bad judgment, boundless courage, and always, always, faith in their power to move mountains.

Few of them lived long enough to discover the snakepits beneath the boulders.

I still think of them as children of the light, the best and the brightest, first to mount armed resistance and first to die in the struggle. Perhaps it was the loss of this whole generation that in some measure accounts for the horrors of Bosnia.

They took me into their tribe, accepted me, adopted me, and I felt happy among them, so much so that I let myself be carried away, blinded by their light. What I failed to see were the others, the children of darkness, more numerous by far.

And much more fertile.

I was also much too busy and self-absorbed to notice my parents' growing despair, but by the end of the year the crisis came to a head: we were rapidly running out of money.

Characteristically, I had until then been kept in near-total ignorance about their finances, such as they were—the derisory amount which Jewish emigrants were legally permitted to take out of Germany, supplemented by a few large bills sewn into coat linings and by some gold coins baked into crisp large rolls. My father had counted on at least a minimal income, but by now he was forced to admit defeat; his chances of obtaining work, let alone a legal work permit, were practically nil. The new régime in Belgrade engaged in an active flirtation with Nazi Germany and was certainly not about to ease the restrictions on refugees.

In any event, we faced a double threat—starvation on the one hand and, on the other, expulsion as undesirable aliens without visible means of support. No relief organization of any kind existed in Belgrade at the time, nor did the Jewish community offer any assistance. We were entirely on our own, and in the final days of the year we had to come to some decision.

Many other refugees who, a few years later, found themselves trapped in similar situations chose to do away with themselves, and they were probably luckier than many who didn't. But in 1934 the level of despair had not yet reached quite that point, and I recall a memorably miserable night in late December when the three of us debated until almost daybreak what to do, although the only real choices we had were to either hang on and take our chances, or else go back to Berlin. In retrospect it seems hard to believe that Jewish refugees could seriously contemplate returning to Nazi Germany of their own free will, but quite a few did so, unable to make a living or a life for themselves in exile.

It was the first time my parents treated me as an equal, and I paid them back by informing them magnanimously that of course they were free to do whatever they wanted, but as for myself, I would under no circumstances go back; I was sure my Yugoslav comrades would help me survive in Belgrade by myself, underground if necessary. The brutality of that proposal is probably inexcusable, but for many of us teenagers caught up in "the movement" our group or cell had in effect become a family far more close-knit and real than the bonds of flesh and blood; moreover, my out-and-out refusal to even discuss the possibility of a return to Germany may have saved my parents from taking a potentially fatal step.

At the same time I came up with at least a partial solution to the dilemma. My mounting revolutionary fervor made me eager to lop off my bourgeois roots and transform myself into a genuine proletarian, and the most obvious way to do this was to quit school and go to work; as a minor under eighteen I did not yet require a work permit. Predictably, my parents resisted, feeling that we were already quite sufficiently proletarianized. But although they discounted my ideological commitment, in the end they had to bow to reality: someone had to earn some money. Still, they balked at my intention of becoming a carpenter's apprentice. "This is the Balkans," my father reminded me; the Stone Age, as far as he was concerned. "Fourteen hours a day, six days a week sweeping floors, shlepping tools, and getting cuffed and beaten whenever you don't fetch the coffee fast enough to suit some idiot of a journeyman or master." I thought he was probably exaggerating, but I couldn't be sure, and in the end we compromised.

Even though he probably employed no more than a hundred people, Geza Kon's bookstore and publishing house were the largest in Yugoslavia, and Geza himself one of the country's wealthiest men. In his lifetime the cultural avant-garde depised him as a vulgar profiteer and archreactionary; today—or rather yesterday, when there still was such a thing as culture in Belgrade—he would find himself enshrined as a great culture hero and eulogized in the most progressive literary circles. I doubt if he would be amused. A sense of humor is not the only sense he lacked; his needlessly gruesome death suggests a certain deficiency in ordinary common sense as well, a not uncommon trait among business tycoons.

Geza was a Hungarian Jew who some time prior to the First World War crossed into what was then Serbia and became an itinerant book peddler specializing in pornography. In those innocently repressive days pornography, coyly referred to as erotica, was published almost exclusively in high-priced luxury volumes accessible only to an affluent clientele. Concerned about their reputation and anxious to preserve a "plain brown wrapper" anonymity, they were forced to rely on the discretion of the booksellers, most of whom exploited their leverage simply by charging exorbitant sums for choice items. Geza, however, had higher ambitions.

Having known him only in his later years as *gazda*, the boss, a grossly obese ogre with a crippled leg who ruled his empire by barks and bellows from a glass cage in the middle of the store, I have trouble thinking of him as having charmed his way into the good graces and confidence of major political and cultural figures in pre–World War I Serbia. Then again, it may not have taken an excess of charm so much as a complicity in corruption, of which there never was a shortage in Serbian politics. But with the establishment, in 1918, of the Kingdom of the South Slavs, which in effect amounted to the extension of Serbian rule over Croatia, Bosnia and Slovenia, his erstwhile clients suddenly found themselves wielding vastly enlarged powers in a vastly enlarged state. And, whether as a reward for discretion and favors rendered or in recognition of his indubitably outstanding entrepreneurial qualifications, Geza was awarded the quasi-monopoly on the textbooks required in schools throughout the new country and in very short order became a multimillionaire.

Making money was his only true interest in life; his meteoric rise as publisher and his posthumous, not altogether undeserved apotheosis as one of the shapers of Yugoslav culture between the wars may, I suppose, be made to demonstrate either the cultural benefits of naked greed or the law of unintended consequences. Books to him were simply a means for making money. He never read anything he published and in fact probably could not have done so even if he'd wanted to, for although he communicated loudly and volubly in both Serbian and German, his command of either language was quite superficial, and I very much doubt if he mastered the literary subtleties of even his native Hungarian. But he published good books—he had a flair for finding, using and exploiting the right sort of help—and he published them because at the time there was in the new country an enormous hunger for good books, with no such thing as public libraries to even partly satisfy it.

An enormous hunger or, as he saw it, an enormous market, the trouble being that most of those potential customers could barely make ends meet and had very little money left over for luxuries such as books. And this was where his creative genius asserted itself—Geza Kon was the first to deploy a sales force that covered most of the country and sold books on the installment plan. He deliberately kept the monthly payments to the barest minimum, so that as little as the equivalent of half a dollar a month could buy not only individual volumes but also many of the sets he later specialized in publishing. He made money on the deal, but he also put a great many good books into the hands and homes of people who could not otherwise have afforded them.

Geza showed up at the Ashkenazi synagogue on the high holidays but otherwise avoided any involvement in the affairs of the Jewish community, rightly fearing that it might cost him some money. Giving a job to a poor refugee youngster, on the other hand, was the sort of thing that made him feel like a philanthropist.

He agreed to hire me as an apprentice and, big spender that he was, to pay me the equivalent of six dollars a month for a six-day, sixty-hour week, which was just about a dollar more than what we had to pay for rent; forced to leave the Hotel Royal, we had settled in a cold-water flat out in the boondocks. Double that amount would have enabled the three of us to live quite comfortably, but Geza was not one to give in to impulsive generosity. For him, charity began at home, as with the block-long Mercedes, the exact replica of the Führer's own, which he had imported from Germany—and which a few years later, during the German occupation, would serve as the Nazi *Stadtkommandant*'s personal conveyance.

In February 1935 I became an apprentice in the Geza Kon Bookstore and Publishing Company.

The huge sycamore loomed by the side of the track, splendid in full summer foliage and even more magnificent in winter, its bare branches tracing patterns of intricate promise against the sky. For thirty years it was a faithful running companion, a dazzling sight every time I rounded the westerly turn, comforting, familiar, yet ever changing. Yesterday it went down, a victim of the freak storm that hit the Island. I feel as though I had lost a friend; the jagged twenty-foot stump surrounded by the pyre of dead limbs and branches evokes the vision of a corpse tied to a stake.

The start of my working life at Geza Kon marked a radical shift in relations between my parents and myself.

It was not until many years later, when I myself had become a parent, that I could let myself sense some of the pain and humiliation they must have felt at being, so to speak, depen-

dent on their teenage son, and at the cost of what they considered his normal adolescence. Upending the balance of the conventional parent-child relationship is bound to have some peculiar consequences. What it did to my parents I'll never know; at
the time I didn't give it a thought, and later we never talked
about it; we were not the sort to scratch each other's soul even
if we did feel the itch every now and then. What it did to me
was abort both adolescent rebellion and ancestor worship. It
would have been as impossible to rebel against the defeated old
man—he was in his late forties at the time—who seldom even
bothered leaving the house as it was to mythologize him into an
all-powerful father figure. Impossible for me, that is; others
reacted differently. Kafka refused to the end of his life to cut his
internalized demon father down to the size of the poor real-life
slob who had married his mother.

By this time we had settled into a two-room apartment way
on the outskirts of town near the end of the trolley line. It had a
kitchen with a wood-burning stove and a bathroom with a tub
and shower, but neither heat nor hot water. The most appealing
feature, an unobstructed view of large open spaces marking the
boundaries of the Belgrade municipality, became a disastrous
liability in winter, with icy blasts sweeping equally unobstructed across the fields, and temperatures dropping into
Siberian ranges. We did our best to keep the cold out by sealing
the windows with newspapers and using whatever furniture
we could spare for firewood. One of the toys from which my
father had evidently not been able to separate was his World
War I cavalry sabre, complete with tassel, and I can still see him
in the kitchen, ineffectually hacking away with it at some
redundant chair leg. I don't know about swords into plough-
shares, but as axes they are pretty damn useless.

In order to report at the store at seven o'clock in the morning I had to leave the house at half past six if the weather was

good enough to use my bike; in winter, with snow on the ground, it took me nearly an hour to cover the distance on foot. Store hours were from eight in the morning to eight at night, with a three-hour siesta from one to four. During the first few months on the job I still dutifully came home during the noon break and after the store closed in the evening. But gradually, as I was ever more deeply drawn into the life and work of the underground youth movement, I remained in town for the siesta, came home later and later at night and eventually got up at 5 A.M. during the summer months to participate in early-morning drills. My parents fretted about my health and lay awake till all hours of the morning, frightened out of their wits, until they finally heard me lugging my bike up the stairs. I have no idea how much they suspected about my outside activi-ties—more, I am sure, than I gave them credit for. But what were they going to do about it? What do you say to your child when he is the one who supports the family?

We had begun to live in two entirely different worlds.

SIX

Herr Weissbart, a middle-aged bachelor and former music critic in Munich, was the only guest at the Hotel Royal who seemed oblivious to the age gap between us. We played a great deal of chess together during the early months of our stay and later continued to have long, animated talks about anything and everything, from politics to movies. He was enormously learned, a born teacher capable of conveying a passion for books and the arts, and like the rest of the refugee crowd he had absolutely nothing else to do. He was also a homosexual, a flagrantly obvious fact which prompted several officious souls to communicate their concern for my virginity and future sexual orientation to my parents. To their credit they not only dismissed these idiotic warnings but made a special point of keeping up relations with "poor Mr. Weissbart" after we moved into our own apartment. He was actually quite well off financially, thanks to a sensitive reading of the political climate which for years had made him deposit his money abroad. To my mother, however, any lone bachelor was ipso facto poor. A principled skeptic, he gently questioned my nascent enthusiasm for the epiphanies of dialectical materialism, which he dismissed as an indigestible farrago of faith and fiction while at the same time lending me a number of books on the subject and encouraging me to think for myself—well-meant advice, but a tall order even for someone twice my age. As I became immersed in the world of my peers we saw less and less of each other, but I remained fond of this particular ideological sparring partner and retained an enormous respect for his tact and erudition. So that his death in January 1935, on my fifteenth birthday, came as a shock.

In a note written before he took a lethal dose of barbiturates, Weissbart explained that the plebiscite in the Saarland region, which took place on January 13 and in which 95 percent of the population voted for affiliation with Nazi Germany, had robbed him of his last glimmer of hope. "Those who kept telling us that the Nazi rule was only based on terror, that there exists another decent, democratic Germany, have been lying to us. That they fooled themselves as well is no excuse, just as we no longer have an excuse for putting our faith in fairy tales about a better world to come."

He was buried as he had requested, without ceremony of any kind, in a remote corner of the New Cemetery, somewhere in the no-man's-land between Christians and Jews where he belonged. Almost the entire refugee colony, about a hundred people, had come to pay their last respects to one who had certainly not enjoyed much respect while he was alive, but hypocrisy is part of proper breeding. And there was more to it: all of them—all of us, I should say, shivering on that windswept hill under a threatening winter sky—had a vague premonition of Weissbart as a pioneer, a man only slightly ahead of his time.

As indeed he proved to be.

At the end of that same year, on December 19, 1935, Kurt

Tucholsky, one of the most gifted writers of the Weimar era, killed himself in his Swedish exile. "The world we worked for and to which we belonged no longer exists. The world to which we belonged is dead. It behooves us to bear this with dignity."

Epitaph for the world of my parents.

In my own world, meanwhile, I reported to the Geza Kon Bookstore every morning at the crack of dawn and learned how to clean and polish miles of parquet flooring. Robotlike, still groggy with sleep, I'd go about spreading and sweeping up sawdust until, toward the end of the hour, all ten of us sorcerer's apprentices would come to life performing a frenzied sort of one-legged skating routine on wooden boards to which pads of steel wool had been fastened. By eight o'clock the sales force and clerical personnel checked in, the doors opened to the public, and the "boys" took their assigned places.

The Foreign Department, in which I spent most of my first year, took up about half the store and stocked a remarkably eclectic collection of French, German and English literature, classical as well as current. Its nominal head was Herr Blumenthal, a frightened and ineffectual little Jew who had lost his job in a Frankfurt bookstore taken over by the Nazis and somehow ended up in Belgrade. He suffered from ulcers, or rather from an ostentatiously non-Jewish nag of a wife dying to return to the fatherland, and moreover he lived in constant fear of his assistant, Mrs. Onich, who never hesitated to express her contempt for Jews in general and for him in particular. Onichka, as no one dared call her to her face, a Viennese Valkyrie made of stainless steel topped by a solid blond wig, owed her name as well as her unassailable position to the Serbian police inspector to whom she was married and with whom Geza had no desire to tangle.

Despite their subsurface enmity, both these creatures jointly conspired to always make me look busy, Onichka out of perversity, Blumenthal because he was afraid of Onichka. We seldom had more than a trickle of customers throughout the day, the bulk of them mere browsers, so that initially I had to spend year-long mornings and afternoons standing around with a feather duster in my hand. The only legitimate excuse for a temporary absence was the need to attend to normal or, for that matter, abnormal bodily functions; there being only two single toilets in the basement, one of them reserved for Geza's exclusive use, the expedition invariably involved a lengthy wait which I eventually learned to put to good use.

I never did acquire the knack of properly wrapping the customers' purchases, but I began to familiarize myself with the literature displayed on the shelves. In that twilight era between the fall of the Habsburgs and the collapse of everything else, the German language still topped all others as the *lingua franca* of Eastern Europe, although the Serbian elite generally leaned toward French; as for the exotic idiom of Anglo-Saxons and shiftless emigrants, it was about as popular as Hindustani. The only English-speaker in Belgrade—English to the extent of not quite being Serbian—with whom I ever tried to commune in that language was my barber, deported from the States as a subversive alien after the First World War.

On the whole, the foreign department reflected that division. It featured a remarkably extensive collection of German literature, including a great many of the writers whose books in Germany proper had already been banned and burned. The French inventory, on the other hand, was top-heavy with sets of the conventional classics designed to grace the bookcases of overage Serbian pundits and upscale civil servants. There was one single floor-to-ceiling case filled with English books, a collection of identical paperbacks that covered the range from

standard classics to the famous or merely notorious British and
American authors of the 1920s. They were the unique product
of an enterprising German publisher, Tauchnitz, who for over a
century published English-language books in inexpensive editions for the preglobal, continental market, in which the origi-
nals tended to be beyond the means of most potential readers.
The sale of Tauchnitz editions in English-speaking countries was
prohibited.

That bookcase intrigued me, for reasons which at the time I
made no attempt to understand. But I resolved to learn English
as soon as possible.

If I were to go to Belgrade as a journalist, with a commission
from a newspaper or magazine to interview Milosevic; and if
I were to obtain an explosive device from a terrorist organization linked to a Muslim country—Libya, Iran, Syria via Bosnian
militants; and if that device were to be concealed in a tape
recorder . . .

Certainly a more constructive way of committing suicide
than taking the gas pipe.

Except that the consequences are unforeseeable and may be
worse than letting the bastard die his own death. As no doubt
the assassination of Hitler would have proved to be, had it been
successful.

Assassins—successful ones, at any rate—are born, not self-
made. One risks ending up a clown in history, like Alexander
Berkman.

What sort of asshole cares about his place in history?

I had naively assumed that even after dropping out of school
I would go on keeping in touch with my new friends, and most
especially the Gypsy, on whom I obviously must have had a
crush of sorts. It therefore came as a blow when, on my last day

in school, he quite coolly informed me that we would no longer be seeing one another. "We make sure to only know the people we need to know," he explained, "otherwise they'd soon put the whole movement out of commission. You're a worker now, not a student. You'll have new friends soon enough. I'll see to that."

Thus it came about that one day, about three weeks into my new life, as I was leaving the store for the three-hour lunch break, I found two rather weird-looking characters waiting for me at the back door. One of them, as broad as he was tall, had the build of an orangutan and the face to go with it; the other seemed frail, with delicate, almost androgynous features. Neither was much given to the social graces of the bourgeoisie— although both, as it later turned out, came from conventional middle-class families and had merely adopted what they conceived of as proletarian manners. But in our first encounter they acted like two surly brats forced to make nice to an idiot cousin from the country, which in fact was pretty much the situation they found themselves in. They asked me, or more precisely they gruffly ordered me, to take a walk with them in the Kalemegdan, and I went. I somehow knew that excusing myself because I was expected home for lunch and didn't like to worry my parents would strike a distinctly sour note and end my underground career before it ever got started.

We were to become close friends, lifelong friends, although this, sadly, is not much of a boast since both Walter and Marko were killed early in the war, barely out of their teens. Walter the orangutan was an apprentice machinist who masked the exquisite sensitivity of a true musical prodigy by outrageously foul language and ostentatiously crude manners. He was ugly to the point of scaring little children, but none of us sensed the depth of despair that his image in the mirror inspired in him because to us who knew him for who he was he had long since come to look perfectly normal if not downright handsome. I was told that he died in a botched ambush of German troops and that his rage outlived him; they had to hack off his hand to retrieve his gun.

The androgynous Marko was an apprentice dental technician close enough to the end of his one-year apprenticeship to have his handiwork inflicted on live patients. Even he himself felt sorry for them, though on the whole he probably did less damage than the actual professionals; the Russian lady dentist with a barber chair and a foot drill in her living room who rinsed her instruments in the kitchen sink and filled my teeth with cotton wads and plaster of Paris was fairly representative of the state of dentistry in the Belgrade of those days. Marko later turned out to be the ideal conspirator, quick and resolute, able to play any role assigned to him. After the German occupation in 1941 he remained in the city, joining a group of Serbian pro-Nazis while helping to organize the resistance. He seems to have done a brilliant job, but success tends to breed the sort of overconfidence of which he always warned others. One night he himself took a chance, violated the curfew as well as his principles and—probably because he had incriminating material on him— tried to escape when challenged by a Nazi patrol. They stood him against the wall and shot him on the spot. *Ordnung muß sein*. He had just passed his twenty-first birthday.

During the trial of Julius and Ethel Rosenberg a witness for the prosecution testified that at one point the Russians had rewarded Julius with an appointment to the rank of colonel in the Red Army. Or so at least he was told by his handlers, who played Rosenberg like a kazoo. But true or not, it enabled this addlepated schlemiel to inflate his tiny ego with one mighty burst of hot air. They look at me, and all they see is just another loser, a little guy who eats shit like everybody else. Whereas in real life . . . But one day they're in for a big surprise. Come the revolution they'll see me marching down the street in uniform, with a big pistol and a chest full of medals. . . .

Bertolt Brecht, *monstre sacré*, knew the feeling. Pirate Jenny, mopping floors, enduring on fantasies about role reversals come the revolution, the power she will have when all is revealed:

> . . . and a ship with eight sails and with fifty canons will bombard the city. . . .
> And a hundred men will go ashore toward noon, and step into the shadow
> And will catch each and every one from each and every door, and put him in chains and will bring him to me
> And ask me: Which one shall we kill?

Julius Rosenberg had a hell of a lot more in common with Jenny the Pirate Moll than with his wife Ethel. He suffered from a bad case of arrested development, infantile rages and emotional constipation. Whether these far from uncommon attributes warranted the death sentence is another question.

It all struck me as uncannily familiar, childish fantasies just like the ones that once upon a time saved my own sanity and self-esteem. Here I am sweeping floors and wrapping packages and jumping when the old bastard barks *dechko jedan*—get me a boy—and I don't dare look at any book by a left-wing writer as long as Onichka prowls the aisles—but if you knew who I really am, how I spend my nights, and what I'm going to do to you come the revolution . . . Nothing much could faze me as long as I was convinced that the worm was bound to turn, that some day *we* would be running the zoo and that I would get even with Geza and Onichka and the Police Prefect who made us cringe and plead for every three-month residence permit.

The worm did turn, much sooner than any of us expected. But not quite in the direction I wanted it to.

As for my parents, I like to think that they eventually got used to my not showing up for lunch or supper or both, that they stopped fretting about my coming home at all hours of the night and leaving at dawn almost every Sunday for all-day hikes regardless of the weather. But I know better, knew better even then, one reason why we were never able to talk about it. I was afraid they would go mushy on me, while they were too proud or too decent to indulge in the sort of emotional blackmail that so many parents practice routinely without shame or hesitation. They felt terrible about my working as hard as I did, they felt sorry for me and for themselves, but above all they suffered from a crushing burden of guilt. They themselves had had to battle the tides through much of their lives—the First World War, the postwar upheavals, the crazy runaway inflation, the rise of Nazism, but they kept clinging to the myth of what they remembered as their own idyllic childhood and adolescence, so unlike that of their only son. They never asked questions about my secret life, and I volunteered few details, but they were bright enough to guess where and how I was spending so much of my time and to be appropriately scared; they never went to sleep before they knew me safely home for what was left of the night.

Both died young. My turn to feel guilty.

There was never a break between us, but we drifted apart, or more precisely, I drifted into an entirely different orbit from which parents were excluded by definition.

SEVEN

The modern youth movement, rooted in the dark night of Teutonic myth, has spawned strange fruit in our own time. Its basic creed, like that of all religions, was a lumpy brew of half-truths, delusions, contradictions, platitudes and wishful thinking, but what really drove the *Wandervögel* out into Mother Nature bellowing folksongs and strumming guitars was the refusal to grow up and face the compromises of adulthood. Two world wars, a holocaust, the H-bomb and the reappearance of the plague did much to discredit the "Ode to Joy" and its fantasy of *Alle Menschen werden Brüder*.

One result was the progressive fragmentation of this children's crusade into innumerable heresies and cults ranging from the original sandaled romantics to Boy Scouts, Hitler Youth, Pioneers, Woodstock Nation, the rebels of '68 and the street gangs of Los Angeles. What they all had in common was contempt for their elders—by whom, as often as not, they were being manipulated from behind the scenes—and the prospect of inheriting the earth. But whereas our generation welcomed the challenge, convinced as we were that we had all the answers and the power to right all the wrongs of this world, the current one seems, by and large, a good deal less naive. Which is both inevitable and unsettling.

The youth movement as a social phenomenon, its impact for good and for evil on individual lives and on totalitarian politics, warrants much more thoughtful and informed scrutiny than the oedipological psychobabble and stale clichés about teenage identity crises it has thus far engendered. But no postmortem analysis can ever hope to capture, let alone convey, the feeling of what it was like to belong to the movement. To belong, *tout court*. To have a faith and a family.

Later on we used to kid each other about it, but that first session with Walter and Marko as my would-be inquisitors was a tense and awkward affair all around. They were barely a year or two older than I, thrown into the breach by their more valuable and more vulnerable elders as a first-line defense against potential infiltrators and all too keenly aware of their heavy responsibility, the more so since I happened to be the first new recruit they ever had a chance to interrogate. Throughout what should have been my lunch hour I sat on a secluded bench in Kalemegdan Park, squeezed in between the orangutan on one side and the delicate, flute-voiced baby Torquemada on the other, who both took my fascist past and my evil designs for granted but were eager to exact a full confession. Oddly enough—and this I recalled a few years later, when news of the first Stalinist purge trials with their improbable confessions began to trickle in— they did succeed in making me feel guilty, except that I couldn't for the life of me come up with anything to confess. There were, of course, my class origins, but then almost the entire "progressive movement," and most certainly its intellectual leadership in those halcyon days of the Popular Front, was afflicted with the same hereditary taint.

In the course of the next few meetings my interrogators gradually unbent; though they were to prove their toughness by the way they lived and died, neither was cut out to be a Chekist or an *apparatchik*. Eventually they gave me a clean bill of health, granted me full absolution and took me to their leader, who proved to be a venerable seventeen-year-old.

The Communist Party as such had been outlawed in Yugoslavia since the early 1920s and its underground organization quite effectively crippled by aggressive police action that combined harsh justice with naked terror; a good many of its top leaders were already serving long sentences in the Sremska Mitrovitsa penitentiary. Some more astute observers, denounced at the time as sociofascists or Trotskyite defeatists, pointed to more cogent reasons for the party's sorry state, such as its fatuous propaganda aimed at an industrial proletariat all but nonexistent in this still overwhelmingly agricultural society, and above all the dead hand of Moscow, determined to exercise absolute control over all internal party affairs via a Kremlin-appointed leadership safely ensconced in Vienna.

But these were the concerns of an older generation, old farts long since over the hill, or over thirty, anyway, people who had screwed up and were now paying for their failures. We were in a much different position, for whatever the party's poor showing within the power structure at large, Communism was the dominant force by far among the country's urban youth. In Belgrade, the vast majority of university and high school students were either militant activists or, at the very least, devout fellow travelers who could always be counted on for demonstrations and other mass actions. Forbidden by law to organize their own movement, they had developed an ingenious, viruslike routine of insinuating themselves into legitimate organizations such as the Boy Scouts or the YMCA and of operating under the cloak of their respectability; thus every May 1 saw massed ranks of Scouts, both boys and girls, head out into the countryside to celebrate the Holiday of Labor, and the sweet-tempered Anglican clergyman who ran the local YMCA never caught on to the fact that the earnest and polite young people meeting several nights a week in the basement were studying Lenin.

I was introduced to something that called itself the Belgrade Chess Club for Working Youth, sponsored quite properly by the Yugoslav Chess Federation and meeting in a dilapidated building by the Danube that had been abandoned by its owners. The narrow lane ending at the river's edge was unpaved and unlit, but the lack of heat and sanitary facilities merely added to the peculiar attraction of this hideaway, the more so since the outhouse offered a glimpse of the far from blue Danube. The rooms had been whitewashed, and the salvaged pieces of furniture added an illusion of clubby comfort. Still, there were several chess boards set up, people occasionally even played, and the bulletin board displayed not only the supposed ranking of the top ten players but also some yellowing bulletins of the National Chess Federation.

Like all conspiratorial organizations, this one was run on the "need to know" principle, so that even the nominal president of the organization and his executive officers, dummies in every sense of the word, were deliberately being kept in the dark as to membership figures and surreptitous activities. That they owed their titles and positions not to their popularity but to their expendability and political innocence was something their self-importance prevented them from realizing until it was too late. In any case, the club was unofficially divided into study groups of about ten to twenty members each. They were warned to go by pseudonyms only and to have as little contact as possible with members of the other groups, but these instructions, spawned by some paranoid Moscow spymaster, proved a joke in this town and among a crowd that for the most part had grown up together.

For over half a year in 1935 I spent nearly every free moment at the club. It was without a doubt the intellectually most challenging period of my life, and one which did more for me than all my formal education put together. The fact that ten years later the overwhelming majority of students hated Marxism— by then an integral part of the syllabus in all Yugoslav schools— more than any other subject is one of those piquant ironies that could teach teachers a great deal about teaching if they were teachable themselves.

For one thing, the Gospel according to Marx, along with anything containing potentially subversive ideas—and that took in most of twentieth-century literature—was forbidden fruit, which of itself added immeasurably to its appeal. The books, officially banned and circulating clandestinely, were treasured, with each copy going through literally hundreds of hands. Reading thus became an act of self-assertion, an integral part of the teenage rebellion, and though it may have served the short-range goal of indoctrination, the unintended long-range effect was to educate a great many youngsters who otherwise might never have cracked a book on their own.

And for another, we ourselves were in charge of running this peculiar institution, all of us teachers as well as students, none over eighteen. The result was a sometimes successful but always exhilarating experiment in learning by doing. Once a group had agreed on the subject to be studied, each member took part in preparing and giving the lectures. The mythology of Marxism was, of course, considered the ultimate revelation, the top of the pyramid; but before these youngsters—most of whom had left school between the ages of twelve and fourteen—could climb that slippery slope and be initiated into the gnosis of dialectical materialism, they first had to acquire some basic concepts as well as some of the history of human thought, which in turn required a broader knowledge of history in general. Imperialism, the intrigues of international conglomerates and the struggle for oil and raw materials made no sense without a background in geography, and any debate about the more abstruse theses of Friedrich Engels had to draw on at least popular science. To be sure, we paid a price for our independence. We often overreached ourselves, and there were times when we could have used grown-ups who knew what they were talking about; I remember one fierce argument we had about dialectics and the Heisenberg Uncertainty Principle that went on until three in the morning and ended in a near fist-fight. Ignorance can be bracing as well as bliss.

But we also tackled many less esoteric subjects. There was sex, of course, everyone's favorite, with my version of Wild Willy Reich as the textbook. And what with one thread leading to another and the warp and woof of knowledge being what it is, we boldly plunged into an analysis of Sigmund Freud, as yet happily unaware of his status as an outlaw *verboten* in the spiritual fatherland of the Working Class. This although when it comes to the politics of what used to be Yugoslavia, Freud certainly proved a far more pertinent guide than Marx.

The leader of our group—or cell, to use the terminology then current—was a skinny, sad-eyed seventeen-year-old whose impeccable manners and gentle ways seemed utterly off pitch in this particular environment. Yovan never cursed and never used dirty language, which marked him as an outright freak, and yet he somehow knew how to make us not only respect but love him.

I certainly did, once we came to know one another. He had grown up in a small town in Croatia, the only son of the local doctor. For a long time he did not want to talk about why he had been packed off to Belgrade in his early teens, to live with relatives whom he hated and to work his butt off as an apprentice in a typewriter repair shop. We assumed him to be an orphan, but in due course—on an overnight hike to Mount Avala, a glorified hill some six miles east of the city topped by the Tomb of the Unknown Soldier—he let slip that his father was still very much alive, a psychopathic drunkard, wife-beater and child-molester. Yovan, trying to defend his mother, had slugged the man with a water pitcher, cracked his skull and vowed next time to finish the job. That was how he found himself on a train headed for Belgrade. His mother died a few months later, but his dad was still the only doctor in town, and some of his patients even got better in spite of him. "Some day," Yovan concluded dreamily as we lay in the grass looking up at the midsummer sky, "I'll go back there and put him out of his misery."

Said wholly without malice, in an almost cheerful tone of voice, and I am convinced that he would have done just that had he lived long enough to grow up.

It was Yovan who first made me aware of possessing a skill enormously valuable to the group, and in fact to the entire organization: I was the only one thoroughly familiar with the language of Marx and Engels. And of Freud, for that matter. This so-called mother tongue of mine which I did my best to disown enabled me to go directly to the source; moreover, it gave me access to a whole range of subjects for which the literature in Serbian was either scarce or nonexistent—a gift unearned, disdained and rejected by me but envied by everyone else, and they were not about to let it go to waste.

That was how I became The Interpreter. May I be forgiven by the phalanx of *Dichter und Denker* whom I vulgarized and misinterpreted, and by my ex-comrades, living and dead, whom I unwittingly conned into taking my word for scripture.

* * *

On the under-the-counter shelves at Geza Kon, hidden from the general public, I had discovered a stock of leather-bound volumes with blank covers. They contained such exotica as a sampling of photographic evidence collected by the sex crimes unit of the Düsseldorf police department, an abundantly illustrated account of sadomasochistic orgies in a Hamburg bordello and the—again amply illustrated—initiation rites of a health-through-sex cult, probably remnants of Geza's past as the resident pornographer. But alongside these symbols of capitalist corruption, which much to my regret I could only furtively glance at whenever my miserable bosses were otherwise occupied, they had had the bad taste of stashing away the last pre-Hitler copy of *Das Kapital* next to this stimulating filth. I persuaded little Blumenthal to sell it to me, discreetly, without Onichka knowing about it, and on a modified Geza Kon instalment plan of ten dinars—about a quarter—every payday. It was the first book I ever bought with my own money. A couple of months later, made reckless by a hundred-dinar raise, I bought Freud's *Introduction to Psychoanalysis*. They were the only two books I took with me when I left Europe. I have them to this day.

With no background to speak of and no one to guide me, I struggled for weeks with the Bible of Communism and the convoluted prose of its founding father. The biting sarcasm of his polemical asides struck me as the acme of sophisticated wit, his prophecies of the inevitable revolution and the better world to come seemed grounded in pure science and hence beyond debate, and—with some assistance from slightly more popular texts—I finally absorbed enough of the Theory of Surplus Value to be accepted as an authority on the subject, so much so that in contravention of conspiratorial discipline I was asked to give my series of talks to several of the other groups as well. And just as I was beginning to consider myself the budding Bukharin of the youth movement, my own cell decided to make further use of my talents and voted to study the teachings of Sigmund Freud.

With Freud I fell into a different sort of trap, but one in which I had lots of company. Leaving aside everything else that divides them, in terms of style and clarity of expression Freud is the antithesis of Marx. The luminous simplicity of his prose—never quite matched in any translation—made it all too easy for me to believe that I fully understood his ideas, but my simplistic version of his basic theories failed to convince my audiences; the suggestion that they might have irrational motives for what they did or failed to do elicited howls of protest, and the whole notion of the unconscious was denounced as idealistic claptrap.

Whereas we were materialists.

In my early days as an embryonic little Marxist I had been puzzled by this contradiction; it seemed to me that we, who were fighting for a better world, qualified as idealists. But it was explained to me that all language is not equal, that some words mean what you want them to mean, and that philosophically speaking an idealistic Marxist was a materialist, whereas a greedy capitalist was an idealist even if he believed in nothing but money. My mentors' grasp of philosophy may have been somewhat vague, but in the end it simply didn't matter. We each of us originally joined the movement for any number of reasons, some of which might even have defied analysis by Dr. Freud; but initially at least, ideology was seldom among them.

EIGHT

Tosha Kovach was Geza Kon's treasurer. It took me some time to find out that this bald-headed penny-pincher, perched on a bar stool at his rolltop desk hard by the main entrance like an overstuffed bird of prey keeping track of every dinar and fraction thereof that entered or left the store, also happened to be Geza Kon's younger brother. He probably had changed his name already back in his native Hungary, where anti-Semitism is a virulent plague endemic since the Middle Ages, but like most such people trying to be what they were not, the only one he fooled was himself. Certainly not the Germans, who right off sent him across the river to be butchered in the Banyitsa camp.

It was Tosha who kept the books, reluctantly counted out the pay to each of us twice a month, always with the sour face that said "This hurts me more than it hurts you, and what's more, you don't deserve it," checked on the cash register several times a day and quite literally kept a tight lid on the petty cash box buried in one of his drawers; trying to get reimbursed by him for a trolley ride to the printer could trigger major hysterics. Yet the stingy bastard did me a good turn, albeit unwittingly, which absolves me from having to simulate gratitude. One morning he came in earlier than usual and saw me get off my bike. I was sure he would bawl me out for being late— "again you're cheating on your employer" was the usual formula—but instead he wanted to know where I had got that bike and if it was really mine; presumably he felt that if I could afford my own wheels, I was obviously being overpaid.

For once, however, this was not what he had on his mind.

Geza Kon's major contribution to Yugoslav culture, as already mentioned, was his sale of books on the installment plan. Out-of-town customers paid by postal money order, but within the capital itself payments were collected during the first three days of each month by a band of impromptu collectors drafted for the purpose from among the lower and lowliest ranks of the personnel. They were each assigned a section of town, and since the results at least in theory depended on how fast they got around, the sight of my bike gave Tosha an idea, always a rare and memorable occasion in his life. On the first day of the following month he himself handed me a list of names and addresses, with the amounts to be collected at each stop; the bike, he growled, ought to enable me to cover at least twice the normal territory.

I cursed the son of a bitch as I set out, feeling like one of Fagin's crew and vowing to pay him back for this humiliation once the wretched of the earth had become the human race. But in the meantime it turned out to be a beautiful summer morning, I was on my own riding my bike all over town instead of being cooped up in the store, and I could have been perfectly happy had I not been near paralyzed by shame. It was one thing to go into the final conflict, quite another to ask someone for money.

I had no rational explanation for the way I felt, which was why, with a singular lack of logic, I blamed it on my "bourgeois" upbringing, as though delicate sentiments in matters relating to money typified the bourgeoisie. At any rate, it is one of those facts of life for which there are no rational explanations, only Freudian ones; the more than half a century I have spent in the land of milk and money may have modified my attitude but not my feelings. This even though my adventures as Geza's bagman were anything but traumatic.

Unforgettable the initiation, a variant on the loss of virginity, in a house in the old Jewish quarter by the Danube around the corner from what used to be my *Gymnasium*. It consisted of a dozen or so tiny apartments, all opening onto an unpaved, barren inner courtyard, and after having psyched myself up by invoking the courage of Dimitrov before his Nazi judges, I rang the bell, bracing for an assault. But the apparition that opened the door, a huge, amazingly ugly woman with stringy black hair, tobacco-stained teeth and an improbably sweet smile, greeted me with unfeigned delight before I ever had a chance to state my case. She wore a flowered housecoat with rhinestone slippers to match, and I doubt if she even bothered trying to understand what I was struggling to spit out. She knew perfectly well why I had come; it wasn't every day that someone rang her doorbell. She caught my neck in the crook of her arm, wrestled me into the sad little room, made me sit down, fed me some biscuits with jam and in the end gave me double the amount she owed me. "And don't you give the boss one penny more than he has coming to him," she warned me. "That old geezer is going to bust. He's already swallowed a thousand times more than he can ever shit out."

The start of a trip through the dark heart of the city, the place beyond the landmarks where people live with their vast loneliness, their venom, their hopes and their failures. And their hospitality, heartfelt beyond tradition; almost everywhere I went they received me like an eagerly awaited guest, offered refreshments and sent me on my way with a generous tip over and above whatever they owed. A young woman who said she absolutely could not pay that month nonetheless insisted on my taking three dinars from her "for your troubles" and got very angry when I refused. Only one old curmudgeon slammed the door in my face, muttering about the fucking Jew bastard and what he could do to himself; nearly all the others seemed pathetically pleased to see me. I cannot believe that they were all loners, perverts and social misfits. On the other hand, who else would buy books, and books at that which they obviously could ill afford?

Every month, after the three-day collection spree, I was treated to tales of epic encounters between horny collectors and nymphomaniac housewives, and though skeptical enough to know them for the lies they were, I kept hoping. One never knows. No harm believing in Santa Claus, or whoever is in charge of these fringe benefits.

I met lots of housewives, but none offered to seduce me.

In the end, all I had to show for three days of pedaling around town was about a hundred dinars in tips and some intimate glimpses of other people's lives that left me uneasy. Tosha counted my receipts without any nasty comments. I took it he was pleased.

How far can memory be trusted?

I can recall at will—or think I can recall—any given moment, scene, face or emotion out of my past. But memory is a treacherous process of creation; how closely does what I remember resemble the reality of what I once experienced?

It took me forty years to get back to Belgrade, a vastly different city from the one I had left in 1938. Over one-third of the total housing stock and at least half of all buildings in the center of town were destroyed in the devastating Nazi air raids of Easter Sunday 1941. In the decades since, the city had slowly recovered, expanded, spread across the Sava river and spawned the chimerical New Belgrade. On the Zemun fairgrounds, where the Nazis and their native allies once slaughtered Jews by the thousands—including Geza Kon and his entire family— there now rose a Congress Center and an Intercontinental Hotel, defiantly pretentious showpieces of the new capital of nonaligned nations. In the old town, on the other hand, recon- struction had been slow and partial; wide gaps remained, con- spicuous like missing teeth, with impromptu little squares and pocket parks filling the void and promoting oblivion. At least half the remaining buildings on Knez Mihajlova Street, once the main drag where I had watched the nightly *corso* from inside the store, were of postwar vintage, while the few older ones had been patched up and altered beyond recognition. But on the first day of my visit I was walking with ghosts, so that the enormity of suddenly standing on the sidewalk in front of Geza Kon's bookstore, after forty years of war, revolution, chaos and Communism, to find it totally and utterly unchanged from the way I remembered it took some time to sink in. It turned out to be neither dream nor nightmare. The building, both outside and inside, had quite simply survived, preserved in reality exactly as it had been in my memory of it.

Everything was in its place: Tosha's rolltop desk by the entrance, the cash register on the other side where Dragitsa, a fat little porker, sucked candy all day, the semicircular desk on which I unsuccessfully struggled with wrapping paper and string, Onichka's perch behind the counter from which she spied on me, the stunning oak shelves throughout the store and the parquet floors on which we used to perform our steel wool war dance. The Tauchnitz editions were gone, and though I did not check under the counter of what had been the foreign department, I assume that the pornography had been repatriated during the Nazi occupation. Other than that there were remarkably few changes; Geza Kon's glass cage had been eliminated along with the boss himself, and the store imaginatively renamed *The People's Bookstore*. Be it said that since then Geza Kon has become the culture hero of the new generation—woe unto the people that needs heroes—and his name once again proudly graces the entrance to what used to be his fiefdom.

My memory turned out to be stunningly accurate, my recollections validated in almost every detail, but that may be as much a source of concern as of pride.

In midsummer 1935 my maternal grandmother (my father's parents both died before I was born) sent word from Breslau that my grandfather was critically ill. Strong-minded and of an eminently practical bent, she quite simply enclosed a railroad ticket with her laconic, factual note.

My mother left that very night for Germany.

It was a time in my life when I had, or thought I had, a rather distant and objective view of her, and her impulsive response struck me as both gutsy and mildly insane. True, the Nazi government still maintained a pretense of pseudolegality while quietly preparing for the apocalypse. My mother had a valid German passport, she looked like a Protestant pastor's daughter, and her reason for making the trip was both plausible and verifiable. But I felt that she was taking a very foolish risk, and though I kept my misgivings to myself, I resented the fact that my father raised no objections.

What I really resented, I now know, was the intensity of my mother's emotional involvement with her own parents; the distance between us, carpeted with eminently civilized respect, did nothing to appease the vestiges of infantile jealousy. Moreover, there was a practical aspect to her trip: the gold coins she smuggled back out in crisp rolls especially baked for the purpose by my grandmother kept us going for months.

Two days after she arrived in Breslau, my grandfather died. He was seventy years old, too young for the Franco-Prussian War of 1870, too old for the First World War, but an ardent German patriot and reasonably observant Jew who saw no contradiction between the practice of his religion and his fervent Bismarckian nationalism. He died of pneumonia in his own bed, unaware of his good fortune; seven years later his seventy-five-year-old widow would be stuffed into a cattle car and shipped off to Auschwitz.

After a month in Germany my mother came back fuming with indignation at the willful blindness and inertia of most of her friends and relatives. Everywhere she went, Jews would assure her that things weren't all that bad: "So what if we can't attend *their* schools anymore; our own are vastly superior. So what if we can't go to the movies or the theater anymore; we have our own." Autonomous Jewish culture in Berlin was flourishing, with an abundance of lectures, concerts and courses. Her relatives in the garment industry were working around the clock making uniforms and, not coincidentally, a fair amount of money which, even if they could not take it out of the country, went some way toward making up for the fact that they were no longer allowed to sit on park benches. At any rate, it severely limited their sympathy for people who deliberately chose the miseries and privations of exile over a comfortable if somewhat circumscribed existence in Germany.

Two weeks after her return, on September 15, 1935, the infamous racial laws were officially promulgated at the Nazi party convention in Nuremberg. After the *Kristallnacht* of November 9, 1938, even our relatives in the garment industry began to get the message. Too late. When they finally did leave Germany, it was not of their own free will. None came back from that trip.

•   •   •

And yet:

Within days of the Nuremberg circus we received a communication from the German embassy in Belgrade that threw us into a tailspin of anxiety. In prose polite but peremptory, a consular official urgently requested my father to come and see him.

We spent a night debating the pros and cons. Chances were that they were going to deprive us of our citizenship and, being their legalistic selves, wanted him to sign a statement testifying to his having been duly informed to this effect. The citizenship they could shove. But its loss also entailed the loss of our passports, for lack of which the Yugoslavs would expel us forthwith, a prospect particularly unpleasant in light of the fact that none of the surrounding countries was likely to admit us; a refugee family had recently spent four days on a bridge in Fiume between Yugoslav and Italian customs until the Fascists had taken pity on them.

On the other hand . . .

Some of these discussions among refugees can only be visualized as an arm stretching into infinity, with an endless number of hands growing out of it on alternate sides and clutching at straws.

Yet whether or not he showed up at the embassy was unlikely to make a difference. And there was always the possibility that it had to do with something else, perhaps even something perfectly innocuous. He didn't want to go in the worst way, but I pointed out that if he didn't, they would probably involve the Yugoslav police. Which tipped the scales. He went.

And came home stunned.

At the embassy he had been received by a midlevel functionary. The man, a career diplomat who had already represented the Weimar Republic in Belgrade and was obviously slated for early retirement, told my father in strict confidence that Swiss authorities were unhappy about Jews seeking asylum in Switzerland but had trouble keeping them out so long as they carried passports indistinguishable from those of Aryan Germans, welcome as always. They had therefore prevailed upon the Nazi government henceforth to mark all Jewish passports with a conspicuous *J*, in effect rendering them useless for crossing almost any border in Europe. The new regulations were to take effect the following month, which gave him three more weeks in which to issue regular passports without the stigma. A quick check with the Yugoslav police had made him realize that our current passports would expire within the next eighteen months. He strongly advised us to bring them in forthwith so that he could renew them for another five years.

He quite possibly saved our lives.

NINE

Winters in Belgrade began in late November and often lasted into April. Now and then the heavy snows would bury the trolley tracks, but given the blessed scarcity of vehicles in town, they caused no serious problems otherwise. For me personally, however, winter was the season of character-building misery. It meant getting up in the dark of night, it meant cold showers in a freezing apartment, it meant—since I could not use my bike—trudging four miles to work at six in the morning and, after cell meetings that often lasted way past midnight, four spooky miles back home through snow-covered, deserted streets, always on the lookout for police patrols who were liable to stop any lone teenager at that hour on well-grounded suspicions.

While I am convinced that being cold, scared and perennially underslept has no intrinsic educational or otherwise redeeming value whatsoever, it did teach me the power of simple, simplistic and simple-minded faith. Even the mere whiff of martyrdom

confers the odor of sanctity, of which smugness is the most
conspicuous symptom. I stumbled about in a perpetual glow,
jaws clenched in grim defiance as behooves a soldier in the
struggle for socialism. What, after all, were my troubles compared to the sufferings of our comrades in the Nazi camps or,
for that matter, in the dungeons of Belgrade police headquarters?

But one morning, just a few days before the New Year, a
rather well-dressed girl my own age whom I had never seen
before came prancing into the store, nonchalantly leafed
through a few of the German art books on display and gradually
worked her way over to where I tried to catch up on some
sleep while alphabetizing a stack of catalogue cards. She
stopped next to me and picked up another book. "How much?"

While I checked the letter code penciled on the inside cover,
she very quietly asked, without moving her lips: "You Karl?"

I nodded. Karl was my party name, a *nom de guerre* not easy
to live up to. Karl Marx, Karl Liebknecht, and now Karl von
Ossietzky, winner of the year's Nobel Peace Prize, kept prisoner
in a Nazi concentration camp. I was preparing a translation of
some of his writings to be read at our New Year's celebration.

"Yovan sent me. They picked up some of our people. The
club is full of cops. Don't go near it. Lie low till you hear from
him."

Two nights later I found Marko waiting for me as I left the
store. "Yovan's been arrested."

The first few weeks of 1936, between a lonely New Year's
eve and a dreary sixteenth birthday, put my entire newfound
faith to the test.

That I was scared for myself goes without saying. My lectures
on Marx, Freud and Wilhelm Reich had earned me an entirely
unconspiratorial prominence, and the true identity of that "brilliant young Marxist theoretician," as I liked to apostrophize

myself while dusting books or sanding the floors, could have remained no mystery to the informers who had infiltrated the club.

But while I at least would suffer for my convictions, my parents would suffer because of me. I had no right to jeopardize their already precarious existence, yet at the same time felt that such scruples were themselves indicative of a sentimental, petit bourgeois cast of mind difficult to reconcile with true revolutionary commitment. It was a preview, at a personal level, of a conflict that haunts all resistance to totalitarian power—duty to one's family versus duty to the cause. During the war it gave rise to agonizing discussions that were anything but theoretical: was it justifiable to assassinate a Nazi officer, ambush a convoy or execute a traitor knowing that dozens, sometimes hundreds of hostages would be killed in retaliation? On the other hand, if action is to be guided by compassion for the innocent, resistance becomes impossible altogether, yet without resistance the number of innocent victims will ultimately be far greater. These arguments raged hot and heavy at every level of the Partisan resistance movement, morality against expediency, long-range ideological goals versus immediate tactical gains, and the resolution always a heartbreak, no matter what the outcome. Few back then could have foreseen history's grim touch of irony, which invariably deflates all sanctified certitudes. Could Milovan Djilas, our idol of a revolutionary in the thirties, have imagined his little son being ostracized in a Communist nursery school because of his father's reservations about Tito's New Class? Came the revolution, and *plus ça change* . . . For half a century the dissidents of Eastern Europe put not only their own lives on the line but exposed wives, friends, lovers and, above all, their children to often intolerable risks.

•   •   •

No one had ever quite figured out what it was that made Andrea Strassberg choose the Hotel Royal as her permanent residence. She seemed to be quite well off, at least she conveyed the impression of real wealth—a wealthy widow, people said, although she herself had never been known to refer to a husband, late or otherwise—and she definitely moved in the upper strata of the Belgrade establishment; every so often the wife of a cabinet minister or of some high-ranking general came to sit with her in the lounge or in the sad excuse of a garden, two or three women dressed with understated elegance oddly at ease among the shabby furniture and the shabby people.

Why someone like her would prefer the sleazy Royal to the respectable Serbian King and resign herself to living among a gaggle of morose refugees rather than mingle with the cosmopolitan crowd in Belgrade's best, in fact its only decent hotel, was a mystery wrapped in a more fundamental enigma: Who really was Madame Strassberg, Andrée to her intimates? Though always accessible and often apt to while away entire days—her days began around three in the afternoon—gabbing with the Royal's regular inmates, she remained coyly guarded about her origins and about her past. From casual remarks she dropped now and then it appeared that she had spent many years living in exotic places—Alexandria, Bombay, Shanghai as well as London, Berlin and Paris; she spoke French, German, English and Serbian, all four of them with an intimidating fluency that made it impossible, at least for us, to diagnose her native accent.

At the Hotel Royal, her affluence, social status and Yugoslav passport put her in a special category all her own. She was a sort of fairy queen to the refugees, for whom she frequently did small favors and who admired her in return, though the admiration was not untainted by malice. Lorna's father floated a rumor about her having been a recently retired *poule de luxe*, a speculation which outraged my mother but may not have been so far off the mark. Though well into her fifties, Andrée still had the looks, along with the kind of cynical wisdom one acquires from seeing a lot of fat, hairy power brokers in their underwear or out of it. High-class hooker or unromantic widow, I suspect that she supplemented her income by working for French and/or British intelligence, both of them feverishly active in the Balkans and generous to a fault with their taxpayers' money.

What strikes me in retrospect is that Andrée must have been at least ten years older than my parents, yet at the time I always thought of her as still a young woman. Expert makeup and expensive clothes may have been part of the magic, but the way her eyes lit up when she talked and laughed and asked questions did more for her appearance than any facials, milk baths or Paris fashions.

Besides, she liked me. When first we moved into the hotel, she found me refreshingly unspoiled—her words—which I took to mean childish and considered an insult. But what it really meant, as she soon made clear, was that she was quite simply bored with most of the grown-ups and really enjoyed drawing me out. And in some curious way I felt safe with her, safe enough even to make a fool of myself and not worry about it. Which was more than I could say for most other adults, including my own mother.

She had invited me to dinner at the hotel, a peremptory summons rather than an invitation, delivered to the store by messenger. The dingy, dimly lit dining room depressed me; it smelled of greasy food and dead hope decomposing.

"How is the job?" she wanted to know.

I had only seen her once since we moved out of the hotel, at another such command dinner, when she tried to talk me out of leaving school.

"No worse than school," said I defiantly, a ritual incantation designed to ward off self-pity. It did not always work.

"Nonsense," she said, with a faint smile more wistful than mocking. "But if that's what you want to believe, so be it. It isn't easy, being a hero."

"I'm no hero," I protested.

"But you want to be. Or feel you ought to be." She had barely picked at her food and now pushed her plate away, lighting a cigarette. "Go get yourself a girl instead. It's time you got laid. And much, much healthier than what you've been doing these past few months."

The meatballs in the Hungarian goulash, not the greatest to start with, turned to rocks in my stomach. Heroic me mumbled something about not knowing what she was talking about, but she cut me short. "Just don't let's pretend. I hate to see you kids being used. You in particular. This isn't even your country or your battle. But next time around it might be your neck. And where does that leave your parents?"

I've always wondered if it was she who intervened on my behalf and vouched, if not for my innocence, at least for my essential harmlessness. No hero he. Was she working for the police or just playing bridge with the wife of its chief? Was informing on the refugees one of her sidelines, and was that the reason she lived at the Hotel Royal?

I like to think that I would eventually have had the courage to confront her with those questions. But I never saw her again. Three weeks after our memorable dinner she abruptly left town. Years later, during the war, I was told that she had settled in Britain and married an Oxford don half her age. My informant was a former Yugoslav Communist working for the British. Or so he said.

A time of anxiety, of loneliness and isolation. There had been traitors among us, and until they were flushed out, everyone not in jail was under suspicion for that very reason. But so, of course, was everyone who *had* been arrested, because the ex-Okhrana experts who ran the Red Squad, though basically stupid, had learned the rules of the game. The Communists, on the other hand, were justifiably paranoid and, like all conspirators, constantly obsessed with unmasking traitors, which involved them in running an institutionalized Inquisition bearing scant relation to innocence or guilt.

Also, however, a time to think. Always detrimental to one's peace of mind and to the received certitudes of pure faith.

Even before the police raid on the chess club and the temporary suspension of activities I had begun to harbor certain distinctly unorthodox thoughts. When, after the murder of Kirov, the first Moscow trials got under way, we had a number of meetings at which adult guest lecturers denounced the murderous clique of Trotskyist agents who had betrayed our beloved socialist fatherland. Nothing about this made much sense to me. The accused were among the founders of the Bolshevist party and leaders of the revolution. If they were guilty of the heinous crimes and bizarre conspiracies to which they had confessed, then the party had been founded by monsters and the revolution led by its worst enemies. If, on the other hand, they were not guilty, what made them confess? Torture? These case-hardened veterans of czarist prisons?

I had another, even more serious problem with all those revelations coming out of Moscow.

In a pile of French paperbacks about to be discarded at the store I had discovered two books by Leon Trotsky—his autobiography, and a collection of his essays—and been totally captivated by them. Here was a Marxist, the first I'd ever come across who could write lucid and straightforward prose. This didn't mean that what he said was necessarily true, but I simply refused to believe that a man who had devoted his whole life to the cause and contributed more to the final victory than almost anyone else would engage in all sorts of diabolical conspiracies designed to undo his own life's work. It made no sense. The truth was that, given a choice between Stalin and Trotsky, I would choose Trotsky any time. The truth also was that by then I had learned enough about the movement to keep that truth to myself.

And finally, something about my talk with Andrée, the casual remark she tossed off about this being neither my country nor my battle, raised some fundamental questions I had strenuously tried to fudge. Such as that in her eyes, and in everybody else's, I was a German Jew.

To my comrades, this was a matter of very marginal interest or importance. Most were truly devoid of bias, and all of them paid at least lip service to the principles of international solidarity. But—and this had taken time to sink in—in the country at large, and even in the city itself, they were a tiny minority of students and intellectuals. In the long run it became quite impossible to ignore the fact that the vast majority of Serbs were fierce chauvinists, hospitable enough to those foreigners whom they considered friends but not inclined to let the likes of me meddle in their business, let alone fight their battles for them.

Teenagers even in the best of circumstances are prone to identity crises, but the one in which I was caught up seemed to me beyond resolution: a German Jew who was no German and not much of a Jew.

Unless, of course, alienation and marginality are themselves perceived as a quintessential aspect of being Jewish.

TEN

Call it consciousness or call it soul, it is the price we pay for being human, and the coin of the realm is fear. Ever since our expulsion from Eden have we struggled to overcome our fear of death by means of myth and magic, sought refuge in visions of divinity, and conceived ever more elaborate rituals designed to propitiate the gods we created. As opium for the people goes, the rationalist pedantry of Marxism was mere lukewarm piss compared to the ferocious firewater fantasies of heaven and hell, of divine bliss and bloody retribution that have been sizzling and seething in the twisted convolutions of the human brain since time immemorial and for which untold millions have been butchered, burned, beheaded. Communism as a religion turned out to be even more of a disaster than Communist economics, and for much the same reasons—it failed to reckon with the dark, smelly side of the human soul. Punishing dissent may be a way of imposing uniformity, but no mere totalitarian regime can inspire fear of eternal damnation, nor is forced labor a productive way of overcoming selfishness and greed.

But there are many reasons why, in the nineteen-thirties,

Communism was the dominant faith—no other word will do—
among Yugoslavia's students and intellectuals, and no man did
more to foster its spread than King Alexander himself when, in
1928, he crushed an age-old, quasi-tribal democracy and imposed
his own autocratic rule after a series of clashes culminating in
the murder of the leading Croat politician on the floor of parliament. He did it, Alexander insisted, to save the country, and the
joke of it is that he meant it. He was no dictator or demagogue
by temperament but rather an autocratic pedant ill at ease with
people, much like Czar Nicholas, at whose court he had been
raised. Alexander was far more intelligent than Russia's doomed
last ruler, but in a crisis he let his instinct rather than his intel-
lect guide him; by suspending parliament and in effect outlaw-
ing all political opposition he inevitably radicalized what was
left of it. Lacking legitimate outlets, dissent and dissenters of all
ranks, ages and persuasions had no choice but to go underground, where the Communist movement provided hospitality,
technical assistance, and a seductive spread of ideals. Tito owed
a great deal to Alexander.

By the end of spring most members of the chess club, including Yovan, had been released, but the club as such was not
about to be revived; conspiratorial routine required that the
cells be broken up and the compromised individuals assigned
to different organizations. Whether Marko acted on party
orders or on his own initiative in taking me to a meeting of the
Hashomer Hatzair I don't know, but I remember my extreme
reluctance; I had no intention of getting involved with a movement that proclaimed itself at once socialist and nationalist.
National socialism was bad enough, but Jewish nationalism?

The whole question of my Jewish identity was shot through
with contradictions which, like countless other Jews in those
days of innocence and illusion, I had been trying to avoid by a

blind faith in universal brotherhood. True, the Nazis made me proud to be a Jew as a matter of principle, but I would have been hard put to explain what my Jewishness—the Jewishness of an atheist who had no use for either race or religion—consisted of. I am not sure that even today, some sixty years later, I have the whole answer, but the quest itself is very much part of it, a quest that began for me in the spring of 1936 with a decidedly unwilling visit to the basement of the Jewish Community Center on King Peter Street, diagonally across from the Hotel Royal. The Center—which, unlike the majority of its patrons, survived the war and continues to this day to serve what is left of the community—hosted a number of Jewish youth organizations which for one reason or another, usually a lack of funds, had no meeting place of their own. Among them, for a very brief time and to the distinct discomfiture of several conservative board members, was the *Hashomer Hatzair*, Hebrew for Young Guard.

The movement was founded in Galicia in the wake of the First World War as a rather anachronistically romantic teenage rebellion against bourgeois values, closely patterned after the guitar-plucking German *Wandervögel* of an earlier age. But the time for folk-dancing and nature worship had long since passed; revolution, counterrevolution, civil war, pogroms, hunger and misery raging in that part of the world soon politicized the movement and redefined its goals. The theoretical underpinnings, a blend of Marxism and Zionism, amounted to little more than an unconvincing exercise in talmudic dialectics; what gave the *Hashomer Hatzair* its unique character were the practical demands on its members for a personal commitment to a radically different way of life. Unlike the Communists, who counted on the revolution to change the nature of man, these youngsters proposed to start by first changing themselves, and in the most revolutionary manner possible—by living a collective life without private property as farmers in a land of their own.

Romanticism come full circle. And the fact that the kibbutz, this most romantic of ideals, also turned out to be the most, if not the only, practical realization of socialism in our time is one of the ironies of history.

As an organization that encouraged its members to emigrate and did not actively concern itself with domestic issues, the *Hashomer Hatzair*, though viewed with suspicion both by the authorities and by the elders of the Jewish community, was allowed to operate in a murky area of precarious legality. The line between them and the Communists was a fluid one; Communists infiltrated and used it as a shelter much as they burrowed into other legally sanctioned organizations, and the movement in turn fought a constant battle to maintain its Jewish soul without sacrificing its Marxist conscience. One of the most dramatic clashes between these two conflicting goals took place at a summer camp in 1936 when a trio of young Serbian—i.e., non-Jewish—Communists, who had been on the fringes of the movement for some time and, like myself, become entranced by visions of the kibbutz as an ideal socialist society, declared their intention to undergo agricultural training and leave for Palestine to join a collective settlement. The final verdict as well as the week-long disputations that preceded it would have done honor to a clutch of medieval Talmudists or theologians. One side argued that the case of the Jews was special, that two thousand years of diaspora and persecution had cut them off from the land and from physical labor, and that the movement's task was to redress the balance and expunge the heritage of the ghetto so that they could once again become a people like any other. The other side wondered, volubly and passionately, how a movement professing to oppose both racism and religion could reject comrades for no reason other than

that they weren't Jewish, whatever that meant under the circumstances. Didn't the kibbutz, by barring them, merely recreate the
ghetto?

In the end it was decided by majority vote to exclude them
not because they were Serbs but because, by accepting non-
Jewish Communists, the Palestinian kibbutz would be draining
strength from the revolutionary forces in Yugoslavia. The duty
of a Yugoslav Communist was to fight for the revolution at
home.

Never mind Ber Borochov and the ideological justifications
for Zionist socialism or socialist Zionism; what intrigued me
was their practical implementation. Socialism in one country
seemed hard to imagine, even if you had never read Trotsky.
But socialism in one commune, with some two hundred people
holding all property in common, practicing free love, engaging
in manual labor during the day and in intellectual pursuits at
night struck me as the ideal life. I was old enough to know that
there would be hardship, complications, struggle, but not old
enough to worry about it; at sixteen, draining swamps or, for
that matter, dying does not really scare you.

Within weeks of my first tentative contacts with members of
the *Hashomer Hatzair* I was ready to share not only the rest of
my life with them but also everything else as well, and eager to
leave for Palestine when my time came.

More accurately, and more honestly: to leave for the kibbutz.
It would have made no difference to me if that kibbutz had
been in China or on the dark side of the moon. Palestine made
sense; it had a history of utopian idealism, and the era of the
British Mandate, in which the fragmentation of power among
hostile parties made for creative chaos, provided a unique
opportunity for radical social experiments. Other than that,
however, I felt no special attachment to a land purportedly
promised by God to some rather distant ancestors of mine,

none of whom had lived there for at least the past two millennia.

Nor has that attitude changed significantly in the intervening years; the attempts by Brooklyn-born fanatics to read the Bible as a real estate contract still strike me as criminally insane. That such starkly rationalist views run counter to the prevailing passions which seem to animate the vast majority of mankind says nothing about their objective truth, but truth in the abstract bears no relation to a concrete reality ruled by myths, monsters and madness. One may sneer, as I did, at the synthetic nostalgia of twentieth-century Jews for the homeland of their biblical ancestors; the fact remains that this is what it took to create a state and revive a dead language.

One of the clerks who typed up the file cards, bills and shipping labels for Geza Kon's installment plan customers got herself fired for immoral behavior; apparently she also took care of a different kind of customer in one of the boiler rooms, sharing the proceeds with the janitor. The scandal broke abruptly one morning. A replacement was urgently needed, and that was how I found myself suddenly promoted from apprentice to clerk.

The few extra dinars—Geza curbed his generosity for fear of spoiling me—were welcome, not so the change from the somnolent boredom of the store, where I had learned to sleep with my eyes open, to the noisy office in the back, where a dozen clerks were kept busy with work which, as I soon discovered, was not only mindless but for the most part superfluous as well. The filing system and accounting procedures had been set up by two fossilized bookkepers steeped in the esoteric practices of the old imperial Austro-Hungarian bureaucracy. They themselves were long since dead and quite possibly buried in some of the thousands of dusty, crumbling files that lined the walls from floor to ceiling, but their spirit continued to infest the place and, like the empire itself, stubbornly resisted even the slightest departure from established procedures. The only other male was the office manager, a sneaky Hungarian who early on informed me that ideas, innovative or otherwise, were not welcome and that in due course, as I grew up, I would come to appreciate the wisdom of doing things the way they had always been done. I am still waiting to grow up.

The dominant presence, however, was Madame Popovich, Geza's personal secretary, a menopausal peroxide blonde with pneumatic breasts and a nasty temper. In view of Geza's crippled leg and elephantine bulk, the anatomical details of the relationship between her and her boss were the subject of much speculation around the shop. The spinsterish Deborah Fischer, who felt herself and her own skills badly underappreciated, claimed that Popovichka never wore underpants and had on several occasions been sighted balancing on Geza's lap, but more dispassionate voices generally ascribed the lady's preferential position to her silken tongue and big mouth.

It was Popovichka who initiated me into the basics of typing, that is to say, she taught me how to put in the paper and what the space bar was all about. The rest she left up to me, and I attacked the old warhorse of an Underwood with the erotic exuberance of a young man having his first love affair with a machine. Those upright manual typewriters were virtually indestructible, and the full force of one's rage and frustration could be let out on the keyboard. The sharp rise in violent crime may well have started with the electric typewriter and been compounded by the proliferation of computers; now that keys can no longer be made to pound platen and paper in a vicarious assault on the enemy inside and out, we need real Kalishnokovs—and real enemies—to do the job.

It did not take me long to find my way around the Cyrillic keyboard, but the idiosyncratic six-finger typing method I developed, though reasonably fast, was also thoroughly inaccurate. This, however, didn't much matter, because Yasna, the young lady who filed the index cards and bills I typed up, possessed only a very rudimentary notion of the alphabet, which rendered the files practically useless in any case. Yasna herself was, of course, more than useless around the office but didn't have to worry about her job as long as she regularly slept with the Hungarian office manager, a surly son of a bitch who within a few weeks called me into his office and for no very obvious reason identified himself as a secret Communist sympathizer, rather like a flasher opening his dirty raincoat and displaying his turgid ideology. Taking him for an *agent provocateur*, I bared my Zionist convictions and was left unmolested thereafter.

I was making an extra two hundred dinars a month, no longer had to polish floors and could start an hour later in the morning. Horatio Alger on his first rung up the corporate ladder. The work itself was inane, so that within a month I was able to finish my quota twice as fast as everybody else even while reading a book concealed in my half-open desk drawer.

That summer I started my love affair with English.

With a textbook and dictionary in the drawer, I was absorbing words and phrases at a great rate, so that within weeks I felt qualified to tackle *Ethan Frome* and *Arrowsmith*—not exactly the most inspired choices for a beginner, but they were soiled copies being discarded and probably served the purpose as well as anything else. Soon I was ploughing through the collected works of Upton Sinclair, whom "progressive circles" at the time considered the greatest living American writer. His fame as the perpetrator of the *Lanny Budd* series still lay ahead, and I was shocked to find on my arrival in the States in 1938 that few of my contemporaries had ever read *The Jungle*, which back in Belgrade was taken to be the classic, authoritative and definitive description of life in the United States. And whenever I had a few dinars to spare, I bought the Paris *Herald Tribune*; I still remember puzzling for days over the word *attaboy* in a cartoon caption.

By the end of the summer I was reading English with relative ease and had a good command of the grammar. The problem, and a particularly sticky one in English, was the pronunciation, which beyond the articulation of individual sounds involves speech melody and stress. It can properly be learned only from native speakers, and while I could not afford lessons, I found that for the small price of a movie ticket I could get a full two hours of exposure to very authentic English—or rather for the most part American—conversation; it was my good fortune that in those days Hollywood still went in for talk rather than special effects and that even the Indians were quite fluent in the white man's tongue. By seeing the same movie several times over, not for the generally insipid contents but for the sound of the language, I eventually managed to pick up enough of the dialogue to mouth it along with the actors. And as teachers go, Edward G. Robinson, James Cagney, Fred Astaire, Paul Muni and Tom Mix were among the most consistently entertaining I ever had.

As it turned out, I was not alone in studying English that spring.

One of Belgrade's more remarkable institutions was the newspaper *Politika*, remarkable because in an atmosphere of growing official repression and unofficial hysteria at both extremes of the political spectrum, a small but energetic staff put out a daily paper which, in spite of limited resources, compared favorably in both scope and depth with some of the best in Europe. Its generally liberal tone represented a pragmatic compromise between the political realities of operating in an increasingly totalitarian environment and the uncompromisingly progressive views of the owner and editor, Vladislav Ribnikar, a Tito friend and supporter even before the Partisan movement was launched.

The paper's best-known foreign correspondent was Vladimir Dedijer, a giant of a man physically and, as he later was to prove, morally as well. Like many children of affluent and prominent Belgrade families, Dedijer even in the thirties was already a Communist, at least by conviction. He later reported from Spain, came home just in time to join Tito in the underground right after the German invasion in 1941 and stayed close to him throughout the war, keeping a daily journal that still constitutes the best history of the Partisan struggle. His wife, a surgeon, was killed in the fifth Partisan offensive, in which he himself sustained head wounds severe enough for him to be evacuated to Italy. After the war he wrote the official biography of Tito, but when Milovan Djilas was tried and sent to prison on charges of heresy, Dedijer despite some ideological disagreements refused to break with an old comrade and found himself ostracized as a result. His own vision of a socialism tolerant of diversity and his desire to speak his mind led him to spend most of his later years abroad.

But in 1936 Dedijer, then *Politika*'s London correspondent, put together a popular English-language course for speakers of Serbo-Croatian, which was serialized by the paper in daily installments and proved enormously popular. For a month or two, all over town people were practicing their basic phrases and vocabulary on each other, but once he got into the finer points of grammar and idiom, Dedijer soon lost much of his audience. At least among the public at large the fad soon passed, to be replaced by more abiding passions.

Such as sex, rape, patriotism, murder, and the honor of the Serbian male, the daily fare of the *Stampa*, Belgrade's other major newspaper, although the word itself seems singularly inappropriate when applied to this sensationalist rag: the *Stampa* contained no hard news to speak of, and its paper was too smudgy and abrasive to be put to the sort of use Belgrade citizens habitually made of newspapers, toilet tissue being all but unknown and unaffordable in any but the most affluent circles. Even Geza Kon regularly cradled a few pages of the much softer *Politika* under his arm as he waddled toward his private john. The *Stampa* was rotten through and through, as corrupt as the Stoyadinovich government which in effect owned it lock, stock and staff, but that did not keep it from consistently topping the circulation of its rival by a wide margin. Blood, fucking, and the historic grievances of Serbia had an inexhaustible mass appeal, and the formula does not seem to have changed in the years since.

In early summer a Belgrade playboy ravished an innocent maiden on a bench in Kalemegdan Park. Pregnant, she tried to induce a miscarriage and nearly lost her life as a result. Her brother, resolved to avenge the dishonor brought upon his family, put four bullets into her feckless lover without quite killing him, everbody wound up in court, and the ensuing trial a few weeks later—justice in those predrug days being swift, if nothing else—kept the outrage of Belgrade's family-oriented citizenry percolating for months. The *Stampa*'s reportage of the trial, expanded by numerous special editions, so inflamed the public that police reinforcements were needed to save the playboy from being lynched. Mass demonstrations demanded death for the perpetrator; his assailant was hailed as an avenging angel, while prurient souvenir hunters and sadofetishists carved up the bench in Kalemegdan Park on which the titillating crime had been committed and saved the pieces.

The fact that the real victim in the case was hardly ever mentioned had nothing to do with discretion or compassion. She quite simply did not count. This was an affair of honor among Serbs.

And while it occupied the little minds of the man in the street and the women in my office, the Olympic Games took place in Berlin, the Popular Front assumed power in France, civil war broke out in Spain, and Leon Trotsky arrived in Mexico.

ELEVEN

Spring again. A bonus, this one, and I am duly grateful. Fifty years ago today, in a muted spring and a faraway country—Augusta, Georgia, 1943—we got married. A week later I was on the high seas, headed for North Africa. And absurdly happy about it. Saddened by the separation, scared of the submarines that trailed the convoy along with the sharks, but glad to be on my way to war. At last.

The cyclic theories of history are no more reputable than any other rickety construct purporting to explain the inexplicable and to rationalize the irrational. Still, history is bound to repeat itself, if for no other reason than that there are limits to the varieties of abominations human beings can perpetrate. Thus the post-Communist world of the nineties bears a sickening resemblance to the pre-Communist one of the thirties, which makes the subtle differences all the more disquieting.

Such as the extent to which the civil war in Yugoslavia has

become a playground for derelicts and degenerates from all over the world, a fact that has received scandalously inadequate coverage. Unsurprisingly so; greed and politics may shape the market-driven media, but the part played by stupidity and sheer ignorance can never be overestimated. With few exceptions, the reporters on the scene don't begin to have a clue as to what is happening in depths that don't meet the camera's eye.

The place that seven years ago hosted athletes from every nation now is crawling with the dregs of humanity—German neo-Nazis, British skinheads, American gangsters, Russian fascists, Afghan freedom fighters, Iranian cutthroats, predatory vermin from nowhere and everywhere. Which side they kill for scarcely matters; each of the warring factions easily accommodates the primitive nailboots AK-47 sort of bestial nationalism that has superseded fascism. Ideology, in any case, has little to do with their presence; the real lure is loot, rape and murder.

These, then, are the International Brigades of the nineties. We have come a long way.

1936 turned out to be a year full of dramatic developments: the Popular Front came to power in France, and Léon Blum, a socialist Jew with humanitarian ideals and all too refined literary tastes became prime minister. The Italian fascists finally brought their war against the barefoot, spear-wielding Abyssinians to a temporarily victorious conclusion and crowned their little Victor Emmanuel emperor of Ethiopia. The Olympic Games took place in Berlin, the Rome-Berlin Axis formalized the marriage of Hitler and Mussolini, and King Edward VIII gave up the British throne for the sake of a different kind of marriage. But to us the one event that dwarfed all others was the outbreak of the Civil War in Spain.

Never since have the issues seemed quite so neatly joined. Spain was the *éducation sentimentale* of my generation, the

battle of good versus evil. Moreover, it conclusively demonstrated the utter lack of political will and vision on the part of
Europe's remaining democratic governments. We—at least most
of us who were young in the thirties—have since gone through
an education of a different, decidedly unsentimental kind and
learned that the issues were not nearly as black and white as
they seemed at the time, although the black remains black;
nothing can retrospectively redeem the Franco fascists, not
even their relatively benign policy toward Jewish refugees during the Second World War. Their Moorish troops, together with
their Nazi and Italian allies, formed the troika of the apocalypse.
But the Republic, betrayed by the West, made a pact with the
devil. A devil disguised as a pipe-smoking cockroach.

It still hurts to remember the wild surge of enthusiasm with
which we greeted news of the first Soviet ship defying the arms
embargo. A purely symbolic gesture; in the long run, Soviet
arms shipments amounted to very little, compared to the aid
Franco received from his allies. But what Stalin did send, and in
lavish quantities, were NKVD goons, political commissars and
professional assassins. In the end he helped to murder not just
the Spanish Republic but the hopes and dreams of a generation.

This, however, took time for us to grasp. More precisely,
some of us eventually realized that the Communists, having
bought into this war, exacted a heavy price in return, which
included the mass liquidation of their opponents on the left.
Others to this day keep the faith and grow weepy about *Los
Quatros Generales*. Willed blindness is hopeless, untreatable
and incurable. Ask a blind fanatic to read Orwell or Koestler.

But in the early months of the war it was in fact a struggle of
the people against the generals, and the thousands of men
throughout the world who volunteered to fight for the Spanish
Republic against Franco's legions and Hitler's dive-bombers
were ready to put their lives on the line in a last-ditch, hope

against hope defense of freedom. Be it said that even the rank-and-file Communists and their fellow travelers, who made up the bulk of the volunteers, cherished dreams and illusions. For which most of them paid a heavy price.

The leadership of the party, on the other hand, pursued its own—or rather, Stalin's—agenda, one aspect of which was power over the foreign volunteers. The networks organized to recruit, screen and smuggle them into Spain were dominated by high-level Communist functionaries, among them one Josip Broz, later known as Tito, who operated out of Paris.

One medieval custom which survived, if somewhat bruised and battered, into modern times was the extraterritoriality accorded academic institutions throughout most of Europe. In principle, the power of the state stopped at the gates of the university, and even in practice the police generally refrained from entering the premises until, with the rise of the totalitarian regimes, such small concessions to civilization became obsolete. But in Belgrade it was not till 1936 that the forces of law and order broke with tradition and invaded the university.

Not without ample provocation.

Founded in 1905 during the reign of Alexander's social and socialist-minded father, it was the first institution of higher learning on Serbian soil. Whereas up to then young Serbs had to get their university education abroad, thus ensuring a professional class culled from the thin layer of economic privilege, the tuition-free university opened up hitherto undreamed-of possibilities for the large pool of economically deprived but intellectually ambitious and aggressive high school graduates from all over the country. The school started out with about five hundred students in a dilapidated building in the center of Belgrade. By 1937, total enrollment exceeded ten thousand, a number of equally dilapidated buildings had been added to the original "Captain Misha's Mansion," and the whole complex had become a hotbed of radicalism, a quasi-independent Communist enclave right in the heart of the city.

The degree to which this must have rankled the increasingly totalitarian regime, not to mention the bloodthirsty thugs of the police anti-Communist squad, is easy enough to imagine. For years, Communist students—the vast majority of the student body—held rallies on university premises, delivered speeches from the balconies and hung streamers with revolutionary slogans from the windows while the cops could only stand by, gnash their teeth and cut off water and power to the buildings until the demonstrators were finally forced to emerge, at which point the police more than made up for their pent-up frustration.

All this changed in the fall of '36 with a rally in support of the Spanish Republic. Prime Minister Stoyadinovich, anxious not only to promote closer relations with Germany but also to emulate the obviously successful Nazi methods of dealing with internal opposition, ordered an all-out assault on the university that marked the end of any pretense to academic freedom in Yugoslavia. Hundreds of students were beaten, dozens tortured and sentenced to prison. But the real bloodletting, which began that summer and was eventually to decimate the student body, had causes far broader than Stoyadinovich's pro-Axis sympathies or the sadistic clowns of the *Uprava grada*'s Red Squad. The first student volunteers who in 1936 left for Spain became heroes and role models to an entire generation. By 1941, however, those ready to die for their ideals no longer needed to travel abroad; they simply—or not so simply—"took to the woods," as the popular expression had it when someone joined the underground resistance.

The chances of surviving an eight-year string of disasters, beginning with the relentless advance of Franco's mercenaries

counterpointed by the paranoia of Stalinist commissars and culminating in four years of hunger, vermin, disease, freezing cold
and scorching heat while engaged in a constant life-and-death
struggle against a vastly superior foe were obviously not very
great. Of the thousands of Belgrade students caught up in these
concentric circles of hell, precious few made it all the way to
May '45, to what for an instant seemed like the victory of light
over darkness. And even of those few survivors, how many subsequently picked the wrong side in Tito's break with Stalin and
found themselves pounding rocks in the penal colony of Naked
Island? No trustworthy figures exist, just rumors, official denials,
and some fast-fading memories. But in any case, the loss of an
entire generation of potential leaders goes far beyond mere
numbers; it probably contributed much more decisively to the
current crisis than those hoary "primitive tribal hatreds" reflex-
ively invoked by pompous pundits simulating omniscience.

Perhaps the most representative figure of this truly lost generation is Milovan Djilas, now at eighty-two an unhappy and
powerless but still keen observer of the political scene. Born in
Montenegro—his "Land without Justice"—in 1911 and already
a dedicated Communist in high school, he came to Belgrade in
1929, enrolled in the liberal arts faculty of the university and
soon gained the reputation of a charismatic firebrand. In 1933
he was arrested, brutally tortured and sentenced to three years
in the Sremska Mitrovitsa penitentiary, which at the time already
hosted the elite of the Communist party. On his release he was
elected to the party's clandestine Central Committee and
became its most notoriously doctrinaire member, the Saint-Just
of the proletarian revolution. During the years of Partisan warfare he was Tito's chief lieutenant; after the victory he became
Tito's vice president and most likely successor, indisputably the
second most powerful man in postwar Yugoslavia.

And in 1953, he quit.

Nothing so extraordinary about an ex-revolutionary's fall from power and his struggle to regain it. Trotsky is the classic example. But there are few recorded instances of a leader in an as yet unchallenged position of power stepping down of his own free will simply because he has come to perceive the very power he wields as intrinsically evil. Djilas, by resigning after eight years in high office and denouncing the hypocrisy of Titoist totalitarianism, proved that, the First Baron Acton to the contrary notwithstanding, even absolute power does not always and inevitably corrupt absolutely. This inspiring demonstration cost him some seven years in prison, in that very same Sremska Mitrovitsa penitentiary where he had served his sentence under the old regime, with the difference that under the new one he was deprived of even such basic amenities as writing paper and heat in the winter.

As a result, he now suffers from rheumatism and has had at least two heart attacks, but he has written half a dozen books, and he is still alive, not only defying probability and his ex-comrades, most of them long since dead, but also challenging a great many hoary platitudes about the nature of courage and probity.

Back in 1936, however, Djilas was known to us only for his legendary courage under torture, his scintillating brilliance, and his insufferable arrogance, the fanatical commissar more Communist than the Kremlin, and brazen enough to attack even the venerable Miroslav Krleza, Croatia's leading novelist and a consistent though not uncritical fellow traveler, for deviations from the literary party line. He also took charge of organizing the recruitment of volunteers for the International Brigades, and as Belgrade students in increasing numbers left for Spain via an intricate international network set up to circumvent the arms embargo, the *Hashomer Hatzair* underwent a major crisis of conscience, a conflict between its Zionist aims and its revolutionary commitment.

In those days of innocence or ignorance, kids of sixteen were deemed too young to go to war, which made the discussion for most of us somewhat academic though no less impassioned. But the older members of the movement, those who had reached the ripe old age of eighteen, went off to a training farm, where they were supposed to pick up the basics of peasant lore and collective living while awaiting their turn for legal or illegal immigration to Palestine.

We had about two dozen such future pioneers ranging in age from eighteen to twenty-one on a farm in Panchevo, a village some ten miles north of Belgrade in the Pannonian plain. It was an area which for centuries had been part of Austria-Hungary, populated by a broad mix of minorities which, despite deep-rooted animosities, had not yet come to think of themselves as ethnic. The land, however, was largely in the hands of Swabian peasants who had settled there some two hundred years earlier and clung stubbornly to their customs, their German dialect and their traditional dress, although in their farming techniques they were competent and up-to-date. One of the more prosperous among them, with fairly extensive land holdings and what in Pannonia passed for a dairy herd, had been persuaded by means of not insubstantial cash payments from the Zionist organization to turn a gang of city kids into peasantry. He did his damnedest; he worked them so hard that by the end of the day they were usually too tired even to read a book, let alone engage in the customary ideological hairsplitting. But the outbreak of the Civil War in Spain shattered this routine. I suspect that some of the prospective *halutzim* still maintained close links to the party or to individual members; at any rate, there was growing dissension in the ranks over whether or not to volunteer for the International Brigades. The arguments often dragged on into the wee hours of the morning, leaving everyone exhausted, and when Erwin Sauer, the combination godfather, slave driver and plantation owner, finally complained about the work—or rather no-work—habits of his chronically underslept crew and threatened to ship them all back to the city, where in his opinion they belonged, it became clear that the situation was spinning out of control and that some definite policy decisions had to be reached. And while the top leadership of the *Hashomer Hatzair* wrestled with the ideological dilemma and strove to reach a solution in accordance with the theory and practice of democratic centralism, I was drafted to placate the increasingly irate peasant who, like most Swabian settlers, didn't speak a word of Serbo-Croatian and had no intention of ever doing so, on principle. I had by then earned a week's paid vacation, and it was decided that I should spend it on what we referred to as our *Hakhsharah*, our training farm.

Error Number One: it wasn't *our Hakhsharah*; it was Erwin Sauer's farm, and he had ways of making that clear to everyone.

Error Number Two: the assumption that he and I spoke the same language. Though we eventually came to understand each other, the regional dialect liberally laced with Hungarian bore no more than a marginal resemblance to the sort of German I was used to.

Error Number Three: the idea that Erwin Sauer would take me seriously as an emissary or negotiator or anything whatsoever other than just one more snot-nosed city brat.

He was a large man, potbellied but massive, with a slight limp, a bulbous nose, and a pair of tiny pale blue eyes that at times made him look like a pig and at others could drill holes into your skull. It took him a moment, when I introduced myself, to realize that I was speaking what I thought was German; but once he did, he countered with a lengthy and rather emotional diatribe, half of which was lost on me, while the other half had to do with his grievances, of which there were many. I was tired. It was the first day of the first earned vacation in my life, a Sunday afternoon; I had hiked the ten miles from Belgrade with a pile of books in my knapsack, but I felt obliged to make some reassuring noises; after all, I told him, I had been sent up here specifically to help straighten things out. At which point the man exploded, though to this day I don't know whether he was barking with rage or howling with helpless laughter. At any rate, once he calmed down enough to be halfway coherent, he gave me to understand that he wasn't going to have one more parasite hanging about the place and that, if I wanted to stay, I would have to work just like everybody else. "Which isn't asking a hell of a lot," he added, by way of a parting shot.

An abandoned barn had been converted into a dormitory of sorts for the twenty-three apprentice kibbutzniks, eight women and fifteen men, the oldest just past twenty-one. Because of the age difference our previous contacts had been limited and superficial, but hearing them quarrel for hours on end while I was desperately trying to catch some sleep should have made me suspect right then and there that either they weren't cut out for the collective life, or that the collective life was not what it was cracked up to be.

The group had, in the parlance of the youth movement, lost its center. Five of the men had definitely decided to volunteer for the International Brigade, three others were seriously considering it, the question being whether they should be cast out of the *Hashomer Hatzair* for left deviationism or go to war with the official blessings of the movement. Arguments about the nature of heresy, sin and grace tend to heat up easily among the devout, and the dispute in this instance—Jewish nationalism versus international solidarity—had a legitimate enough basis, but the stridency of it shocked me. Had I understood Freud rather than merely read him, I might have guessed that the tensions and personal animosities had a lot more to do with libidos on the loose than with the battle on the Ebro.

During the week I spent on his farm, Erwin Sauer and I got to know each other. I discovered that the man was not just shrewd but also a good deal more intelligent than seemed evident on first contact. He occasionally read a newspaper, listened to German broadcasts, and unlike most of his neighbors made an effort to keep up with farm news and innovations in the field. What he, in turn, found out about me was that I would make a lousy farmer, a prediction about which I was not inclined to give him much of an argument at the end of a twelve-hour day in the broiling sun, in the course of which I got stung by wasps twice, nicked by a scythe and had a plough horse step on my toe. But in one respect he proved more dense than he had any right to be.

The second day out he invited me to share the noonday meal with his family. His wife, he said, wanted to meet a real Berliner, though I suspect that it was his sons—three of them, with the identical nutcracker faces and flat heads—who prevailed upon him to take me at my word and have me convey his complaints to the Zionists back in Belgrade.

Most of them were petty gripes. He didn't like the girls to wear tight shorts in the field, he had caught a boy and a girl in the hayloft in the middle of the day—it wasn't clear whether he objected to the combination, the place or the time—and he couldn't stand the way they talked the nights away and kept falling asleep all day. His real grievance was money. The damned Zionists simply didn't pay him enough to make it worth his while. "You know," he said, leaning across the table and putting a huge, hairy paw on my forearm in a gesture of fake bonhomie, "I bet you there are some cheap Jew bastards among those Zionists."

Sauer and I had some lengthy and not uninteresting talks during what remained of the week. It turned out that *Reichsdeutsche*, as he called them—Nazi agents, in fact—had been busy throughout the area stirring up anti-Semitism and inciting the *Volksdeutsche* here as everywhere to demand autonomy pending reunification with the Reich. They had never liked Jews anyway—blood-sucking hunchbacks with long noses and fat bellies who cheated peasant widows out of their last cow and would rob the alms box if given half a chance—so that the Nazi propaganda fell on fertile ground.

I valiantly tried to make the case for the Jews and to explain to him what the Zionist Organization was all about. He listened politely. He didn't want to antagonize me; he was counting on me to get him more money for his charges. But he steadfastly refused to believe that any of them were Jewish. "The closest a Jew ever gets to the land is to buy and sell it." As for me, well, the way I handled the horses made him wonder. "But you don't talk like a Jew," he insisted.

If he survived the war, Sauer along with millions of *Volksdeutsche* went *Heim ins Reich*, back home to the Reich, though not quite the way Nazi propaganda may have led him to envisage that return.

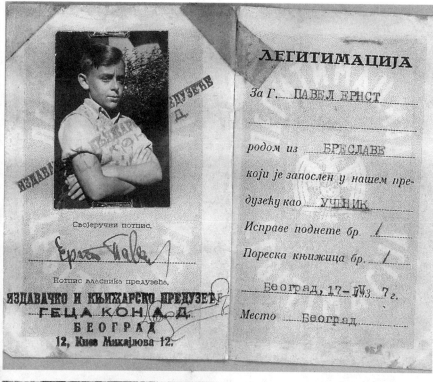

ЛЕГИТИМАЦИЈА

За Г. ПАВЕЛ ЕРНСТ

родом из БРЕСЛАВЕ

који је запослен у нашем пре-
дузећу као УЧЕНИК

Исправе поднете бр. 1

Пореска књижица бр. 1

Београд, 17- IV 3 7 г.

Место Београд

Својеручни потпис.

Потпис власника предузећа,

ИЗДАВАЧКО И КЊИЖАРСКО ПРЕДУЗЕЋЕ
ГЕЦА КОН А Д.
БЕОГРАД
12, Кнез Михајлова 12.

1. Ernst Pawel's Yugoslav
passport (1937).

2. Ernst Pawel in Belgrade.

3. Hashomer Hatzair (1937).

4. With personal friends from the youth group, c. 1939.

TWELVE

Holocaust memorials are apt to evoke highly ambivalent feelings, and the opening ceremonies of the Washington museum have done nothing to lessen my aversion to these institutionalized displays of synthetic emotions. Elie Wiesel's speech was an especially painful example of the sort of drippy sentimentality that vitiates true feelings; and at that his memories, at least, are genuine and earned even if his zeal for self-promotion tends to cheapen everything he does with and about them.

The bitter irony—and imbecility—of inviting a Franjo Tudjman, reincarnation of the Ustasha spirit and self-declared anti-Semite, to the opening ceremonies while no one represents the Serbs who, whatever their failings, lived in peace with their Jews for some five centuries. But monumental stupidity is to be expected from these monument builders bloated with the schmaltz of their self-importance.

Altogether, there is something thoroughly ghoulish about the whole Holocaust industry, conceived in sanctimony and promoted with special fervor by the academic establishment. A Chair of Holocaust Studies, granting Ph.Ds in Auschwitzology and Masters of Bergen-Belsen, with undergraduate courses in Majdanek and Treblinka. How long till we sell T-shirts with "Eyes Get In Your Smoke," or Ilse Koch lampshades made of imitation skin?

Lest we forget?

The dilemma is real, because the dead must not be forgotten. For their sake and our own, but not because their deaths can teach us anything other than that millions of people can be butchered under the most appalling conditions without anyone lifting a finger to help them; *that* lesson has already been absorbed, as Bosnia so graphically demonstrates.

Then again, I may just be living in the prevideo past. Perhaps the Disneyfication of the Holocaust on the Mall in Washington, with its stark realism and its electronic gadgetry, will make it possible for a generation crippled by visual overload and bereft of imagination to get some sense, however vague, of how individual human beings get caught up in the riptides of barbarism and inexorably swept out into the sewers of history. And no matter what the Jews like to believe, you don't have to be Jewish to be a victim.

At least I'd like to think so, though I fear that these kinds of memorials do little more than boost the egos of their sponsors.

The electronic gadgetry inadvertently makes an additional point we miss and dismiss at our peril: nine million dead in less than four years also represents a major breakthrough in bureaucratic efficiency, a tribute of sorts to the German genius for organization, and all of it accomplished the old-fashioned way, with no tools more sophisticated than mere pen and paper. How many more millions could they have processed had they been able to computerize their operations?

We may yet get to know the answer.

*   *   *

Gray skies, intermittent rain and a lingering winter chill in the air at Terezin, eerily appropriate to the mood of the occasion. Fifty years ago the place was both a stage set and a staging area. On the one hand, the Potemkin village filled with happy Jews designed to fool the inspection team of the International Red Cross (easily fooled), fool the Jews assembled here from Prague and points all over Europe (who guessed the truth but clung to hope as a way of keeping alive), and perhaps also to enable some of the Nazis, those with stumplike vestiges of a human conscience, to fool themselves. And on the other hand, staging area for the slaughterhouses to the east. From here, the cattle cars, stacked to the roof with their loads of doomed souls and broken bodies, left for Auschwitz, Majdanek, Treblinka.

The camp, a former fortress built to stop the Prussians, was sanitized by the Communists, turned into a shrine commemorating the Czech resistance, such as it was, with only incidental references to the Jews. The nearby town of Terezin itself, the "ghetto" proper, remains a gruesomely depressing place, a nightmare vision of disconsolate emptiness haunted by ghosts. Thirty thousand Jews died here, well over a hundred thousand were shipped out from here straight to the gas chambers and crematoria. This is where Kafka would most likely have ended up, to share the fate of his three sisters and their families.

This is where both Ruth and I would have ended up, fifty years ago, in these same dreary streets flanked by flaking, shit-yellow buildings. What saved us, what saved most survivors, was sheer dumb luck, not always recognized as such.

For instance:

Whereas nowadays a pharmacist's job consists chiefly of transferring ready-made pills or potions from large containers to smaller ones, filling a prescription back in the thirties, before the advent of the miracle drugs, usually involved compounding it from basic ingredients and often rolling the pills by hand. Professionals with the requisite training and experience happened to be in certifiably short supply in Belgrade, so that early in 1937 the authorities granted the owner of the pharmacy on Monument Square, the city's largest, permission to employ one foreign pharmacist, with the understanding that he would be granted permanent work and residence permits.

It so happened that there were just two refugee pharmacists in town at the time. But whereas my father had spent many years as a paper pharmacist, auditing prescriptions for a health insurance organization, his rival had actually run a pharmacy in Frankfurt until the day he was forced to leave. Understandably enough, they chose the man with the more recent practical experience and damn near broke my father's heart; I don't think he had ever wanted anything quite as badly as that job, which would have enabled us to live in comfort. The lucky winner moved into a private house, hired a servant, enjoyed all the privileges of a legally employed alien with a good income in a cheap country, and had no incentive to get out in time. Four years later he, his wife and two teenage children were murdered when the Nazis took the city.

Lest anyone draw undue comfort from this uplifting tale, let me disabuse them: there is at least equally convincing anecdotal evidence to the effect that more often than not a disaster is just a disaster. Most clouds *don't* have silver linings.

By 1937, a fortunate few of the refugees with means still sufficient to bribe the consular personnel of some South American or Caribbean banana republic were getting out, headed for more exotic venues overseas. But those who remained—a few thousand in the country as a whole, chiefly in "European" Zagreb, but only a few hundred in Belgrade—found themselves trapped, running out of money, forbidden to work, yet unable to escape because every border in Europe was by then hermetically sealed against Jews without money.

Except for a social occasion now and again I had little contact with them; given my schedule, it was rare enough that I saw my own parents. Most of the original settlers still squatted at the Hotel Royal, gradually resigned to spending the rest of their lives in that increasingly disreputable dump. They all seemed to have aged a decade or so in those two or three years since they first came to Belgrade. Lorna's was the only success story of sorts; snugly ensconced in an ultramodern and expensively furnished apartment of her own, she provided escort and other services to affluent but lonely businessmen, and her Yugoslav passport even enabled her to accompany them on trips all over Europe. Yet she paid for her success in the end, with the tight, slim-waisted figure rapidly melting into wobbly flab and the features coarsening under a layer of garish war paint to the point where, barely into her twenties, the *poule de luxe* was already beginning to fade into the battered old whore she was bound to turn into unless she had the brains to make enough hay to provide for a peaceful old age. She didn't have the brains, but it would have made no difference; she was not yet thirty when, passport or no passport, she and her family perished in the death camp on the old Zemun fairgrounds.

I visited her a couple of times after she moved into her own apartment, right near the Geza Kon store. She was as sweet as ever, but I, the ardent champion of the wretched of the earth, had in the meantime become a first-class intellectual snob put off by her mind-numbing banality as much as by her mascara. I stopped visiting her, which did not stop her from sending me a farewell note the day we left Belgrade. Another stone added to the guilt bag.

By and large, however, the outcasts bore their fate with what at the time seemed to me a remarkable degree of stoicism and philosophical detachment, though in retrospect I realize that it was apathy above all, incipient rigor mortis. Six, seven years of enforced idleness spent in the solitary confinement of exile are bound to sap the will to resist; all too many of the refugees were losing their hold on life long before the deportations began in earnest.

Some time early in the year Geza Kon, again pioneering a novel cultural trend, had bought out a small but important publishing house and, along with an impressive backlist, for the first time acquired an in-house editor with solid intellectual credentials. Svetozar Lazarevic had founded *Kosmos* with a vision of publishing the giants of Western thought, but after bringing out about a dozen remarkably handsome volumes—Spinoza, Bergson, Darwin, Spengler, among others—he ran out of money; his books were too expensive for a fanatically culture-conscious but cash-poor market, and he lacked an adequate distribution system. Geza Kon's sales force and his credit plan helped to solve both these problems.

One condition of the takeover, however, was Lazarevic's right to continue publishing *Kosmos* volumes under his own imprint, and in particular to complete his most ambitious project to date—the first Serbo-Croatian translation of *Das Kapital*. It was a daring coup, a brash challenge to a violently anti-Marxist government, and it seems unlikely that without Geza's high-level contacts and judiciously distributed "consultation fees" the two massive volumes could ever have been openly sold. But quite aside from the controversial author, who at least was safely dead and buried, there was the problem of the even more controversial translator who, though far from dead, had for years been buried in the bowels of the Sremska Mitrovica penitentiary, where he was serving a fifteen-year sentence for subversion while translating Marx as a labor of love and teaching himself Chinese on the side.

Mosha Pijade was born in 1890 into a Sephardic family whose roots in Belgrade, as he tactfully used to point out to his comrades, went back further than those of most Serbs. A surrealist painter, writer, and inveterate bohemian, he spent the years before the First World War in Paris, and in 1918, carried away like so many of his fellow artists and intellectuals by his enthusiasm for the Russian Revolution, joined what eventually became the Communist Party of the newly formed Kingdom of Yugoslavia. In 1925, he was sentenced to fifteen years for subversion and illegal propaganda.

A slight, physically clumsy little man with an enormous walrus mustache, an acerbic sense of humor and a quick, restless mind, Pijade had already transformed himself into one of the party's top experts in Marxist theory; prison gave him a chance not only to further advance his own education but also to organize and lead a kind of graduate seminar for his fellow political prisoners. Among them happened to be the future chairman of the party's Central Committee, Josip Broz, alias Tito.

Tito's turbulent life as a soldier and professional revolutionary had given him ample practical experience but thus far left him with little time for theoretical studies. He, too, was determined to put the serendipitous peace and quiet of the prison to good use by making up for the gaps in his education, and Mosha Pijade became his intellectual mentor. The close ties that developed between these two wildly disparate characters, the brilliant but sketchily educated Croat mechanic and the crotchety, sophisticated Jewish intellectual two years his senior, continued throughout the war and lasted until Pijade's death in 1955. He was politically obsolete by the time he got out of prison in 1938, an expansive and anarchic Old Style Bolshevik in a party taken over by young, ascetic Stalinist apparatchiks à la Djilas, but he withstood the harrowing rigors of four years of Partisan warfare, retained Tito's confidence in a series of postwar positions and in the end received a solemn state funeral as Hero of the Nation.

The relative freedom which political detainees enjoyed in the prisons of the semifascist prewar regime not only afforded them unique opportunities for self-improvement but also taught them how to run a jail, when their turn came, in which such humanitarian lapses would not be allowed to occur. In the thirties, when Djilas served time in Sremska Mitrovica, he and his fellow prisoners were able to study subjects ranging from Marxism to Chinese calligraphy; twenty years later, locked up by his ex-comrades in the selfsame prison, Djilas was permitted neither books nor writing materials. Would Mosha, I wonder, have protested had he still been alive?

Be that as it may, by the time Lazarevic joined Geza Kon in the spring of 1937, Pijade had completed his translation of *Das Kapital*, Volume One, and batches of galley proofs kept making the rounds over and over, from printer to prison to the editor's new office in an apartment house next door to the store. Lazarevic was becoming visibly frayed around the edges; educated in France, he had only a smattering of German, a distinct disadvantage when it came to arguing with a master dialectician about the often extensive and expensive corrections which Pijade habitually scrawled in the margins and all over the reverse of the galleys. When Geza first proposed that I might be of some help, Lazarevic demurred: Don't send a boy to do a man's job, he said, or something to that effect. In the end he reluctantly gave in—Geza saw no reason to go to the expense of hiring another body if he already owned a cheap one that more or less filled the bill—but we never warmed to one another. Lazarevic looked down his very prominent nose on me as a brash, semieducated teenager, I considered him a pretentious snob who not only knew no German but also didn't know the first thing about Marxism. We probably were both more right than wrong. Still, I enjoyed the work as such while it lasted, and somehow or other we got it done. Marx rolled off the presses and became an instant bestseller, although in deference to wishes from the highest quarters in the land the sales force received explicit instructions not to sell *Das Kapital* to army officers. Which may explain the army's lack of preparedness four years later, when it came to facing the German attack.

In the meantime I faced a personal crisis of my own, the eternal conflict between lust and duty.

Glibness is all. In today's world, a nodding acquaintance with a broad range of largely irrelevant topics, coupled with the ability to sound authoritative about them, makes you a TV anchorperson if you've got the hair to go with it. Back then it was regarded as symptomatic of leadership qualities. This, I suspect, along with the lack of any more suitable candidates at the moment, was what accounted for my being chosen a group leader in the *Hashomer Hatzair*; even though a relatively recent convert, I already spoke fluent Zionist.

The position of group leader in the youth movement combined the responsibilities of teacher, coach, platoon sergeant, role model and father—or mother—confessor, a substitute, in short, for the parents and other adults we so deliberately and disdainfully kept out of our hair and our lives. In the normal course of events I would have been given a group in the twelve-to-fourteen age bracket and worked my way up, but it so happened that the leader of the oldest group had just received his draft notice, and I was judged best qualified to take his place even though my charges were all more or less my own age.

There were a dozen of them, five girls and seven boys. Two

of the boys still attended school, the rest all had jobs of one sort
or another, and one of the first things I did, this being early
spring and my having absorbed a nasty portion of Prussian acid
with the bluish liquid that passed for milk in my childhood, was
to get them out into an empty field by the Danube at half past
five in the morning three days a week for calisthenics and cross-
country running. I was warned by my more experienced fellow
leaders that "you can maybe pull that sort of thing in Berlin
with a bunch of little Nazis-to-be, but not in Belgrade, not with
these kids."

They were wrong.

The morning workouts became so popular that pretty soon
the younger groups also clamored to be included, which led to
some acrimonious ideological debates among the leadership. It
was pointed out to me that the *Hashomer Hatzair* was not a
sports club, that we were trying to build minds rather than
muscles, and that in any case getting up at five in the morning
was a shock to the nervous system of children under twenty-
one. Someone even cited a local doctor's opinion to that effect.
But we continued to meet through most of the summer, without however neglecting the mind; evenings, after work, we met
to study Hebrew, Marx, sex and history along with a few sub-
sidiary topics or just talked the night away—gossip, politics,
dreaming out loud . . .

I was adequate as a coach and did my best as a teacher, but I
was totally unprepared, at seventeen, to handle the intense
emotions, the complex rivalries and passionate loyalties that
this emerging collective identity was bound to arouse, let alone
function as the substitute father figure the situation called for.
Playing rabbi to my congregants and dishing out sanctimonious
advice was easy, and still seems to me a lot easier than it is
made to appear. Providing emotional support to kids badly in
need of it proved much more difficult, mostly a matter of just

being ready to listen. But keeping my own emotional distance and steering clear of painful entanglements turned out to be utterly impossible. The group was like a family, and you don't step into that pot of glue without getting stuck.

Specifically, there was Vera, one of the girls in my group.

Chronologically about half a year younger than I, in most other ways about twice my age, she had a talent approaching true histrionic genius when it came to dramatizing her personal problems. Most of them were nonetheless real enough and had to do with the clash between a spirited youngster and a depressing excuse for a home. The father, a mean little twerp twisted by failure, lived on the charity of a cousin who employed him as a part-time messenger, the mother took in sewing, and Vera herself, the older of two daughters, had been made to quit school at fourteen and worked as seamstress for yet another cousin—cousin being a generic and in the circumstances rather meaningless term; the thirty or so Sephardic families that originally settled in Belgrade had, through centuries of intermarriage, become one hopeless tangle of a tribe which, while willing enough to socialize or do business with Serbs or even Ashkenazi Jews, would disown their daughters if they married one of them. It was, in fact, only Vera's generation that for the first time openly challenged the peculiar blend of ignorance and bigotry that passes for tradition, and she for one was made to pay for it dearly. When she first joined the youth movement, her father used to track her to the meeting place, drag her out by the hair and file charges against anyone trying to protect her. This particular form of harassment stopped after he was cornered by some of our older boys and given to understand that, although too stringy for *chevapchiche*, the popular Serbian mincemeat patties, he would do fine for fish bait. But the tension at home became unbearable to the point where Vera ran away twice and was branded a whore by her parents.

That these two gnarled, hideous misfits could have produced a child as gorgeous as Vera defied belief as well as genetics, and voicing my suspicions on that score taught me my first lesson in the art and science of pastoral counseling, which is to shut up. I, on the contrary, in response to one of Vera's articulate outbursts against her father, tried to be helpful by questioning his role in her biological makeup and damn near got my eyes scratched out for suggesting, as she put it, that her mother had slept with an Albanian.

I had suggested no such thing. She looked much more Gypsy than Albanian to me, with her coal-black hair, flashing black eyes and a smile that could melt glaciers, but by then I had already learned my lesson and knew better than argue. Nevertheless, she let it be widely known that she hated her new group leader, and that was how we came to fall in love.

It was pure wild, virginal passion on my part, and I like to think that she really grew fond of me, although what tempted her to begin with was the game of ensnaring and monopolizing this pompous little man-to-be who was getting altogether too popular with the rest of the group. She was sixteen, a woman with a past, old enough to get married, and at the same time a troubled and deprived teenager who badly needed someone to talk to and someone to love her. We started meeting every day in Kalemegdan Park during the long siesta hours, quite publicly at first, a group leader in earnest conversation with one of his charges, and gradually moved to more secluded spots as the relationship progressed.

It seems to me that of all the revolutions in our time, the sexual revolution is the only one to have had a moderately positive impact on people's lives. AIDS, of course, has added an altogether new dimension to the problem, and I am under no illusion about video porn and safe-sex candor making for happiness in human relations. But in an age when condoms are being passed out in grade school and oral sex becomes a hot topic on TV talk shows, it may be helpful to recall the good old days of thunderous silence on the subject, when ignorance was what kept virgins virginal, teenagers had no access to contraception, "getting caught" was a fate worse than death, and abortions, for those who could afford them, were performed by snaggle-toothed witches on kitchen tables covered with newspapers.

As for our own attitudes, the main emphasis was on enlightenment—helpful, though scarcely the panacea we took it to be. The illustrated manuals by Reich, Hodan and other pioneers of sex education went a long way toward familiarizing us with the bare facts of life, but the integration of technical know-how with the emotional ramifications of adolescent sex turned out to be a lot more difficult than in my innocence I had anticipated.

There were, however, other complications that lent this particular relationship the bittersweet flavor of an illicit affair. Some had to do quite simply with being young and poor. No way could I have made myself walk into a pharmacy to ask for condoms, nor for that matter would they have sold them to a minor. Furthermore, we had nowhere to meet in privacy indoors, and while alfresco love can be great fun in season, it has its drawbacks. An older friend at work helped with the condoms, but we never had a room of our own.

Yet in a way the more formidable obstacles to the course of true love were of our own making. First of all, the *Hashomer Hatzair* had an ironclad rule against sex in the diaspora. It was argued that the risk of pregnancy and premature family commitments might induce people to stay put right where they were rather than return to the ancestral soil, and like all rationalizations, this one contained a grain of truth. There was, however, a distinctly irrational, ritualistic component to the movement's radical asceticism which, along with diaspora sex, banned liquor, neckties, social dancing and formal academic studies. The resultant conflict of conscience I found easy enough to live with, but once the affair got to be public gossip, it rapidly turned sour. I ceased to be effective as a leader, the group became demoralized, and I offered to resign, but Vera beat me to it. From one day to the next she quit the movement, left home, wrote me a touching thank-you note from Sarajevo, followed two months later by a postcard announcing her forthcoming wedding.

I suffered. But not until I read Proust some years later did I realize that I was not a freak and that others, too, take great pleasure in enjoying the miseries of a broken heart. (I probably could have learned this just as well from watching soap operas; a whole industry is based on that discovery.) As for Vera, she escaped to Albania when the war broke out, was saved by the Italians and eventually ended up in Brazil with her fourth husband, making this a story with a rare happy ending all around.

THIRTEEN

Our first volunteer to leave for Spain was Little David, a gangly giant from Sarajevo who never went anywhere without his guitar. He was huge, in fact freakishly tall for a Sephardic Jew, a head taller than everyone else to begin with, and his forever untamed mane added another couple of feet to his height, but despite a Dickensian childhood in a Jewish orphan asylum he seemed afflicted with an almost morbidly cheerful disposition. Ideology meant nothing to him; he was for the poor and against the rich, and he was a Zionist because, homeless as he was and always had been, he felt that all people, including the Jews, were entitled to a home of their own. But this somewhat ostentatious naiveté masked a quick and quirky mind. Little David could hold an audience spellbound for hours with his jokes and stories, and he made up songs with the effortless ease of the born poet. Yet most of his songs dealt with peace, love, and the brotherhood of man, and it seemed hard to picture him picking up a rifle and killing people when he quite literally refused to even kill a fly.

"This is us against them is what it's all about," he explained, not very articulately, but expressing the feeling we all shared. "I just got to go."

Some time in the early months of 1937 the supreme national leadership council of the *Hashomer Hatzair*, ten aging adolescents in the sunset of their teens, had met in Zagreb and in a turbulent two-day session reached a Solomonic compromise on the subject of Spain: the movement would neither encourage nor discourage comrades from joining the International Brigades, but those who did so would remain members in good standing. Little David, who at nineteen had for nearly a year already been living on the training farm and been next in line for a certificate to Palestine, came to Belgrade instead to make his final arrangements for the trip to Spain, assuring everyone that he would nonetheless see them "next year in Jerusalem." We had become somewhat friendly during my stay in Panchevo, but he startled me when, at a farewell party we threw for him, he asked if he could meet my parents before he left. He had never met any German Jews, he explained, adding somewhat sheepishly that, for that matter, he had never actually got to know a real family of any kind.

My parents?

It seemed a bizarre request. In the movement we had never paid much attention to parents, our own or anyone else's, and although open warfare was relatively rare, we made it our business to keep our distance in every way possible. I had on occasion been forced to meet some of my friends' parents and reluctantly exchanged a few noncommittal platitudes if that proved unavoidable, but why would anyone want to meet my own parents, who didn't even speak the language? Little David, however, was insistent, and since you don't deny a potential martyr his dying wish even if it embarrasses the hell out of you, I arranged for him to have dinner with us in our tiny kitchen.

To this day I don't quite understand how they managed to communicate so well, but the fact is that they never stopped talking all evening. He asked all sorts of questions about their past that would never have occurred to me, they asked about his childhood and about the parents he had never known, and I sat there feeling like an idiot, deservedly so. Every now and then I helped out by supplying a word or interpreting a phrase, but as the talk grew ever more animated, they managed miraculously well without me. I discovered that my father actually knew a lot more Serbian than I realized, my mother spoke pretty good French, and Little David, though he had never gone beyond sixth grade, had picked up a smattering of half a dozen languages just by learning the folk songs. Besides, he had a rare gift for mimicry and one of those faces that speak volumes without the need for words.

Next day a whole group of us, trying to be conspiratorially inconspicuous, went down to the station to see him off, and during the few moments we had to ourselves he tried to tell me that I was lucky to have parents. "Smart ones, at that, and well educated."

They, in turn, were both pleased and moved. He was the only one of my friends they ever got to meet, but if that troubled them, they never said so.

In all, more than a dozen members of the Yugoslav *Hashomer Hatzair* ultimately fought in the International Brigades, and about half of them survived. I don't know what became of Little David, except that he never got to Jerusalem. Not next year, nor ever.

By the spring of 1937 the situation in Spain had deteriorated to such an extent that it took an act of faith to still believe in a Republican victory. The Franco forces advanced on all fronts, took Malaga, leveled Guernica and set up a naval blockade that

choked off the vestigial trickle of arms and supplies to the
Republic. In France, Léon Blum resigned, and the Popular Front
all but collapsed. The Japanese drove ever more deeply into
China and sank a U.S. gunboat. Worst, for those of us who managed to retain a certain critical distance from our own illusions,
was the news out of Moscow. The witch-hunt continued, a
catastrophic eruption of institutionalized paranoia. In January,
Karl Radek and sixteen more of the Bolshevist Old Guard were
put on trial and liquidated as pro-Nazi conspirators; next it was
Bukharin's turn, and finally came the announcement that Marshal Tukhachevsky, commander-in-chief of the Red Army, had
been found guilty of treason and executed along with a substantial part of the Soviet general staff. Under the circumstances, it
took willful blindness to retain one's faith in Stalin and the
Soviet Union, which was why all over the world people firmly
closed their eyes so as to keep reality from intruding on their
dreams.

But we had problems closer to home. The Yugoslav government concluded a Treaty of Friendship with fascist Italy, its
archenemy, and inched ever closer to the Berlin-Rome-Tokyo
Axis. In May, the publisher of the *Politika* was forced to fire a
number of "progressive" members of his editorial staff, among
them Vladimir Dedijer, and replace them with reliable reactionaries. Fascist goons, the future cadres of the World War II
murder squads, became increasingly conspicuous; generous
Nazi subsidies enabled them to expand their propaganda activities and to produce a flood of anti-Semitic pornography.

Given the circumstances, it came as no surprise that Police
Headquarters, the supreme arbiter of our fate as refugees and
foreigners, was giving us more and more trouble about renew-
ing the quarterly residence permits. Not that they had ever
been anything more than grudgingly indifferent, but their
bureaucratic and, under the circumstances, not unwelcome

detachment was now beginning to curdle into outright hostility, and once again it took willful blindness not to see the handwriting on the wall: we were not wanted. The Yugoslav government, whether on its own initiative—the enemy of my friend is my enemy—or under pressure from Berlin, was clearly determined to rid itself of the anti-Nazi refugees.

Many of whom panicked, besieged foreign embassies, dropped frantic pleas into oceans of indifference while as many others shrugged their shoulders, shut their eyes and retreated into their nightmares. But ultimately they all came to feel equally helpless; whether stoically resigned or still frantically thrashing about, they knew that their fate depended on forces utterly beyond their control and that there was nothing they could do other than hope and pray. They were not, as a group, much given to either hoping or praying.

In June it was our turn. I came home late one night to find my parents still sitting up, my father puffing away, grim-faced, while my mother gave me that I-told-you-so look I had come to both loathe and fear. As a congenital pessimist, she always expected the worst; and when it came to pass, as inevitably it did, she felt both vindicated and crushed, the vindication giving her grief an edge of infuriating triumph.

With our current residence permits about to expire, my father had gone to police headquarters to have them renewed and been curtly informed that they would not be extended beyond the expiration date. A local lawyer, friend of a friend, agreed to appeal the decision at once but despite personal contacts never got beyond an assistant inspector, who turned him down cold. No exceptions, he was told; we had to be out of the country by the end of the month. Which gave us about two weeks to come up with a safe haven.

That very afternoon my father had written to his sister, a

refugee living in New York, explaining our plight and asking her to do what she could to secure the financial guarantees we needed to obtain a U.S. visa. It struck me, it struck all of us, rather like addressing a letter to Santa Claus, North Pole, and expecting a miracle by way of an answer, but in addition we faced a more immediate problem: even a miracle would, under the best of circumstances in that pre-electronic era, take several months at the very least.

I was all of seventeen years old, feeling considerably more grown-up than I do now, but underneath the carefully culti- vated veneer of worldly cynicism I must have preserved a sound portion of more age-appropriate naiveté; I don't know what else could have given me the idea and the nerve not only to walk into the lion's den but to beard the lion himself. Some- how or other I apparently clung to the childish notion that a strictly rational explanation would elicit a strictly rational response. And so, come morning, I dragged my father to police headquarters, asked for an appointment with the Chief Inspec- tor in charge of Alien Supervision, and after an hour's wait we were ushered into the imposing office of a frog-faced, elderly bureaucrat whose horn-rimmed glasses gave him a pseudopro- fessorial look.

He listened rather distractedly as I tried to convince him that our U.S. visas were already en route but that it would take a few more months to complete the formalities. It was a litany he had obviously heard before, but when I referred to "my father," he suddenly got intrigued; he had evidently assumed that I was merely acting as interpreter.

"What do you mean, your father—your natural father?"

He had not thus far bothered to look at the passports on his desk. Now he picked up mine and studied it for a moment. "How the hell did you learn to speak our language like one of us?"

I refrained from telling him about translating Wilhelm Reich or giving lectures on the theory of surplus value at clandestine gatherings of subversive organizations, and my becoming modesty must have made a favorable impression. At any rate, he called in his assistant, made me once more parade my unaccented Serbian, and ordered him to extend our residence permits to the end of the year.

A mere few years later, my comrades in the *Hashomer Hatzair* faced some ethically far more complex decisions, but back in 1937 they still had a flat-earth view of the world. They not only failed to appreciate my dilemma but couldn't understand what there was to agonize about. They simply took it for granted that I would go underground and hide out on the training farm until my immigration to Palestine, legal or otherwise, could be arranged. As for my parents, they would have to look out for themselves; after all, they'd had their turn at life.

I, on the other hand, never seriously brought up the possibility of our going our separate ways. At the merest hint, my mother declared that without me they would not consider going to the U.S. or in fact anywhere else and didn't care what happened to them, and I knew she meant it. Committed though I was to the movement, to the people in it and to the ideal of the kibbutz, I still could not conceive of abandoning what I then thought of as my aging parents, although this lofty stance was probably nowhere near as noble and unselfish a sacrifice as I endeavored to make it appear even in my own eyes at the time. For one thing, the three of us were very close, despite the emotional firebreak that created a certain protective distance between us. And for another, I was desperately eager to see America. Not the immigrant dream of streets paved with gold, but the immigrant nightmare of *The Jungle*, the America of the Wobblies, of Sacco and Vanzetti, of Debs and Emma

Goldman, the Wild West of cowboys and Indians, Gopher Prairie's *Main Street* and the slums of Harlem—in short, that continent beyond belief and imagination of which I had caught so many fragmentary glimpses in books and in movies. They did not add up to any cogent vision or recognizably human landscape, least of all a country in which I would want to spend any part of my life, but rather a place of terrifying and at the same time fascinating dynamism, and I was ready to do almost anything just to get to see it once with my own eyes before settling down to the equally terrifying sobriety of collective living.

America, however, still loomed remote in the summer of '37, a shimmering mirage on the horizon, and it seemed most unlikely that we would ever be able to scale the formidable paper ramparts designed to keep us out, let alone actually make it all the way to the distant shore. We had as yet given no thought to any alternatives. Europe was out of bounds for Jews without money, Shanghai didn't bear thinking about. My father fantasized about Biro-Bidjan, Stalin's gift to the Jews, but the fortuitous absence of a Soviet embassy in Belgrade made it impossible for him to act on his impulse. Serendipity once again.

But ready or not, we were definitely outward bound, leaving town or being made to leave, destination unknown, and the certainty of this being my last summer in a place I had come to more or less consider home lent a special intensity and a touch of sadness to the nights, many of them spent out in the open, camping by the river. Time seemed brutally foreshortened, except for the eternity of somnolent afternoons in the office, and I precociously plummeted into a severe midlife crisis. Seventeen already, I felt that much of life had passed me by and that I had grown very old very fast without ever having really been young. It struck me that after more than three years in what George Bernard Shaw called the most beautiful country in Europe—I was on an Irish jag at the time, Shaw, Wilde, Synge, and hunting for a book by a man named Joyce, which Karl Radek had denounced as a microscope trained on a dungheap—I had seen almost nothing other than Belgrade, a town of which one could grow as fond as of a grandmother's wrinkled face but which could scarcely qualify as beautiful in any conventional sense of the word. I owed it to myself, by way of a farewell to the Kingdom of Bloody Myths and Lost Causes, to get on my bike and tour at least some of its more spectacular sights.

Grudgingly, Geza Kon granted me a month's leave of absence. Without pay, *bien entendu*. He had come to rely on me for a host of routine services, and besides, he disapproved of vacations on principle, but he was shrewd about people and may have sensed that I was ready to quit altogether if he turned me down. I didn't even have to burn my bridges; they were about to collapse anyway.

Picking a team of fellow bikers for a trip through the Slovenian mountains down to the Adriatic and along the coast on to Dubrovnik turned out to be a lot more difficult, but natural selection eventually took care of the problem. At first the entire group was clamoring to come along. No one else, however, owned a bike, half of them had never even sat on one, so that in the end there were only four of us left. The other three borrowed bikes, we pooled what little money we had, took a deep breath and were on our way.

The effects of prolonged malnutrition have been extensively documented, but what three weeks on a steady diet of bread and stolen apples will do to the body and soul of an adolescent engaged in strenuous athletic activity has never, to the best of my knowledge, been scientifically investigated.

Our own experiment along these lines was strictly unscientific and in fact wholly unintended, but to blame poor planning would be giving us far more credit than we deserved. Nothing about that loopy voyage went according to plan for the simple reason that as a matter of both principle and teenage hubris we refused to plan anything in advance but instead forged ahead mindlessly from one disaster to the next, each funnier than the last. Or so we thought; whether this had to do with our offbeat sense of humor or with the way a surfeit of sour apples affects brain chemistry remains an open question.

It started with the financial aspects of the operation. Kibbutz-style, we commingled our funds and entrusted their management to Ruben on the assumption that as the son of a bank clerk he had inherited certain useful proclivities, as indeed he had: he warned us beforehand that our total assets barely covered our train fares and that what money remained wouldn't keep us alive for more than a few days. Unimpressed by such petit bourgeois calculations, we bought our tickets to Jesenice, in the heart of the Slovenian mountains some fifty miles beyond Ljubljana, and departed with what small change we had left.

Our first discovery, after collecting our bicycles at the other end and setting out on the road to the sea, was the total irrelevance of maps. A bit of a red squiggle less than half an inch long translated into a mere twenty kilometers, but twenty kilometers up a serpentine mountain road would have taxed even experienced road racers. On our team, I was the only one who regularly rode a bike, and even my practice was confined to city streets; the others had engaged in little more than an occasional spin around the block.

Next we discovered that there was a downside to mountains as well, and the slower the way up, the faster the way down. It takes good brakes and great skill to keep control of a bike heading down a steep road full of twists and turns. We had neither the skill nor the brakes, but some occult power in heaven or hell must protect idiots bent on self-destruction; although we all cracked up any number of times, no one got seriously hurt, and the only casualty was one front wheel turned into a figure eight. Why this struck us as hilarious I no longer recall, especially since paying a village blacksmith to repair the damage further strained the budget.

We soon fell way behind schedule, bruised, battered, sunburned but gloriously happy, moving at our own pace through a dreamscape of snow-capped mountains, meadows and forests that made our preoccupation with time, life, death and other petty concerns of urban existence seem altogether remote. Progress had not yet caught up with that part of the world. Cars were still rare, the streams unpolluted, and except for some stray sheep or an occasional herd of cattle we had the roads to ourselves. The few villages we passed through seemed nearly deserted, the men out in the fields, the women keeping out of sight behind shuttered windows, their truculent suspicion complicating even such simple transactions as buying bread. In fact, the closest we came to a human encounter was a Gypsy encampment, a dozen wagons parked by an icy pond, the women busy doing their laundry while sinewy, barefoot urchins scrambled all over the rocks in search of trouble and the men lay in the shade, resting up from their wives' labors. The tribe seemed much looser, more open than the semiurbanized Gypsies on the outskirts of Belgrade with whom we were familiar and whose unapologetic addiction to petty crime and prostitution made it difficult to romanticize even the stunning beauty of some of the girls. Borders meant nothing to these nomads, but apparently they came from Rumania bound for Italy, and for a lively few hours we had fun getting them to teach us the rudiments of Romany. They seemed both good-natured and fiercely proud, an unstable mix of childlike naiveté

and age-old guile, appealing to the point where we felt tempted
to pitch our tents among them for the night, but in the end bias
prevailed in the guise of caution. Property may be theft, as
Proudhon preached and the Romanies practiced, but we still
needed our bikes, and the girls were just aggressive enough to
make us worry about the clap and our manhood.

Having to live on bread and whatever fruit we could pick
along the way greatly simplified the camping routine; no need
to cook, no need to scrub mess gear. Not until we reached the
coast after a week on the road did we treat ourselves to a single, never to be repeated or forgotten meal of spaghetti as well
as to a hot shower at the Union Hall in Crkvenica. The ride
along the near-deserted coastal highway was easy work after
the scramble through the mountains, and we took our time,
stopping several times a day for long swims in the still crystal-
clear waters of the Adriatic Sea. By the time we reached Split,
we realized that we were too far behind schedule ever to make
it all the way down to Dubrovnik and turned north instead,
ending up in Zagreb, where we took the train back to what still
felt like home.

The bearded Irish virgin was right for once: Yugoslavia—"the
former Yugoslavia," as we now refer to it with ritualistic piety
(like "the former Soviet Union" or "the late George Bernard
Shaw")—was paradise on earth. Why is it that every goddamn
paradise has to be infested with snakes?

Even the Bible doesn't tell us, but merely notes the fact.

A few weeks after I got back, we received affidavits of support from three different relatives in the U.S. The female dragon
who in effect ran the sleepy consular office in the American
embassy was probably a red Russian dressed in white, but those
were pre-CIA days and she also happened to be gruffly efficient. A mere half a year later, after the Nazi annexation of Aus-

tria, tidal waves of would-be immigrants besieged U.S. consulates throughout Europe, but in the fall of 1937 things had not yet come to a head. We expected a long delay as our application was examined and the affidavits duly verified. Instead, the consul waved his magic wand, the dragon typed out the visas, stamped and affixed our photos, and we found ourselves back out in the late fall sunshine, dazed by the sheer improbability of it all.

FOURTEEN

Columbus has been maligned; he *did* discover America. His America. As did millions of others who came before and since, natives and immigrants alike, including those brought here against their will. What they all had in common was the shock of nonrecognition, of facing the otherness of a world not new so much as starkly different from the India they hoped or feared to find.

My own vision of America, part of the baggage I brought with me when I debarked here one cold January morning in 1938, was an eclectic mix of movies, books and biases that began to fade almost at once. In fact, the first glimpse of the New York skyline and the Statue of Liberty, familiar icons the world over, was also my last glimpse of a made-in-Europe fantasy land now vanished beyond retrieval, not only because time distorts memory but also because in 1938 an ocean separated the continents, whereas today the world has collapsed into itself like a dying star and you arrive in New York before ever leaving Paris.

Immigration and customs made for some anxious moments; no European of my generation will ever confront a uniform with total equanimity. Besides, I worried about the three volumes of *Das Kapital* that were also part of my baggage. But after a few desultory questions we were formally admitted to the United States and proceeded to step out onto Manhattan's Twelfth Avenue, at the time a not atypical patch of American soil. The real voyage of discovery, however, began in the cab heading uptown, and is now into its sixth decade.

Although for several more months I struggled loyally to fool myself into believing that America was a mere detour on the way to Palestine, the kibbutz already lost me that very first afternoon at the Bloomingdale branch of the New York Public Library. Streets paved with gold would not have impressed me in the least, but thousands of books on open shelves were a temptation of an altogether different order. They included—as I quickly established—dozens of titles whose possession back in Belgrade would have meant jail or worse; here they were available for the asking. Even more incredible, admission to this treasure trove was free of charge and involved no waiting, no red tape. Nothing, I think, ever had a more immediate and more drastic impact on my view of America than the new library card and the half dozen books I took out with it on my first day in this country. It symbolized a freedom I had never known in my life. That this freedom falls short of perfection in so many ways became clear in due course. And yet, first impressions count; they contain truths of which familiarity later makes us lose sight.

The other defining moment in my relationship—or ongoing affair—with this country occurred five years later, in Camp Gordon, Georgia, where I was probably the only soldier who didn't know how to a drive a car, a deficiency which by army logic

ideally qualified me to drive a truck. After about a day's worth
of instruction I was given a load of uniforms to deliver, an operation that among other subtleties involved backing up to the
sliding doors of the supply room. Lacking any feet-on experience in the delicate maneuvering required, I went strictly by
the book, shifted into reverse, put my foot on the gas and—predictably—backed the two-and-a-half-ton monster in one end of
the shack and out the other, pretty much wrecking the place.

By a miracle, there were no serious injuries—idiot's luck,
once again—and everyone took it as a huge joke, including the
CO, who merely suggested using a tank next time to avoid dent-
ing fenders. What the hell, it was only money. Not ours, either.

Criminal insouciance, of course—lax discipline, irresponsi-
bility at the command level, depraved indifference to government property, inexcusable levity, willful deception. An army
that laughs at screwups, rewards incompetence, hails stupidity,
never forgets that to err is normal and corrects for error by officially reporting it as brake failure. An army whose scandalous
profligacy reflects the unthinking generosity of abundance.

A mirror of the country. Not perhaps of the country at its
finest, but at its most civilian. My kind of army, my kind of
country.

The army has long since turned pro, and the country has aged
by a century or two, but I am grateful to have known it at a time
when both were run by inspired amateurs with a sense of humor
who didn't take themselves too seriously. Except for Patton and
MacArthur, who would have been happier with the Huns.

Somewhere in the course of the five years that lay between
these two epiphanies I ceased to be a European, without therefore running any other identity up the flagpole. This although
the melting pot was still very much the dominant myth, with
newcomers expected to jump into the simmering stew, angli-

cize their names and make like White Anglo-Saxons of whatever
religion, as long as it was Protestant. Many did, and made fools
of themselves, though no more so than their offspring, today's
militant ethnics who go scrounging through the trash bins of
history in search of edible roots.

Our first priority was finding work, problematic enough
even for natives; in 1938 the depression still lingered, and
unemployment persisted until the war broke out in Europe.
Refugees, of course, faced additional handicaps, apart from
common prejudice. An altogether disproportionate number of
the men were professionals lacking the background, language
skills and licenses necessary to exercise their professions. Many
of my father's fraternity brothers—ex-lawyers, judges, dentists,
academics—sold Fuller brushes, encyclopedias or life insurance, or at least tried to do so; their salesmanship was not, as a
rule, up to American standards. Others, especially the physicians among them, struggled to pass the qualifying boards
while their wives worked as seamstresses, cooks, or household
help. We happened to be lucky. Within a week my father found
a job in a pharmacy, which he kept for the remaining seventeen
years of his life. It made my own search a little less desperate
but no less grim. I was one of an army of unemployed
teenagers, with no marketable skills, no work experience and
not even a high school diploma. The only distinctive asset I possessed and tried to put to some use was a knowledge of Serbian, and that was how I eventually got involved with Dushan
Popovich and his *Serbian Daily*.

Popovich was a little man in every sense of the word, except
for a mouth bigger than the rest of him—about five feet tall,
tough as old shoe leather, all wrinkled skin and mean bones. By
then well into his seventies, he had physically come to the U.S.
in the 1890s, worked as a printer and raised a family but in
spirit never left the old Kingdom of Serbia. His printing plant

on West Thirty-ninth Street, in the heart of Manhattan's garment center, must have prospered at one time; when I first wandered into the cavernous, windowless loft I was impressed by the two large presses and the eight linotype machines, not immediately realizing that, like Popovich's Kingdom of Serbia, they were relics of a glory long since past, aside from being mortgaged thrice over. The ailing economy, combined with the combative homunculus's temper—he was known to have thrown hot lead slugs and make-up mallets at argumentative customers—had pretty well killed his business, and by the time I entered my Faustian bargain with him, the only ones still faithful to his open shop were the gangster publishers of a nonunion cab drivers' weekly and the editors of a bankrupt student newspaper at New York's City College. In addition to a permanent cash flow crisis, Popovich also had to contend with a wife twice his size who was in the habit of conking him over the head with a frying pan whenever he came home drunk, which no doubt accounted for the grease-stained protective headgear he never removed even when tempers and temperatures in the shop reached the boiling point. But no matter how drunk, battered or broke—and often enough he was all of these at the same time—Dushan Popovich had somehow managed to put out the *Serbian Daily* five days a week for well over thirty years. It had cost him a fortune and undermined his health, but he considered it his sacred duty as a Serbian patriot to defend his country and the Greek Orthodox faith against the lies and libel of the Papist Croats. This, in his own eyes, more than justified stealing the necessary paper stock from his two remaining customers and pawning his daughter's violin to pay for the postage. He had long ago lost his last typesetter and been forced to print the paper himself, but age, arthritis and liver trouble were sapping his strength, and he was beginning to despair when, as he put it, God heard him and sent help.

The fact that I picked the name out of the phone book does not argue against divine guidance, although had I known that the total circulation of the *Serbian Daily* consisted of fewer than two hundred former subscribers and that the ads were mere space fillers no one bothered to pay for, I might never have taken the trouble to try to track down old Dushan, who often had difficulty navigating the route from home to work after a night of bibulous patriotism and seldom showed up until late afternoon. But the day he found me waiting for him, he almost wept for joy. It was manifestly easier to teach me how to operate a linotype machine than to teach a typesetter enough Serbian to handle the Cyrillic alphabet, and we quickly came to an understanding: he would teach me all about printing, and I would put out the *Serbian Daily* as soon as I was able to, at which point he would pay me twenty-five cents per galley of printed matter. He still owes me thirty-six dollars.

The old man's Serbomaniacal fanaticism lent a touch of lunacy to the experience; he could harangue me for hours on end about the perfidy of Catholics in general and Croats in particular. At the time I ascribed it to senility. Now I suspect a virus endemic to the old sod.

Still, he was a competent printer, and he did teach me how to set type, make up a page, and run the press, after which I took over the editorial function as well by translating the news summary and some of the front page articles from *The New York Times* into Serbian every morning, though I am sure none of the involuntary subscribers ever looked at the paper. I never made any money on the job, but at least I learned the rudiments of a trade that soon came in handy as a social asset of sorts.

Significance lies in the eye of the beholder—who is afflicted, as often as not, with myopia or tunnel vision. Ask any optometrist. (Who, of course, will try to sell you a pair of glasses.) What struck *me* as significant about New York—which at the time I forgivably mistook for America—was something that would have escaped the notice of most normal-visioned people altogether.

Never mind skyscrapers and automobiles. The real contrast in the landscape, from my perspective, was the total lack of an independent socialist opposition in Belgrade as against the Trotskyism rampantly fashionable in New York. In Yugoslavia, Stalinist ideology and the Communist Party apparatus so totally dominated intellectual life and the politics of the left that critics and opponents, especially anti-Stalinist Marxists and other dissident radicals, found no outlet for their opinions and were effectively muzzled, unable to make themselves heard even though by 1938 the chasm between Soviet practice and Communist ideals had not only become grimly obvious but clearly unbridgeable.

The situation in New York was radically different. To be sure, the scene had its share of brainless apparatchiki and brainwashed fellow travelers, who blindly stumbled after their pathetic Browder as he zigzagged from one pile of ideological dogshit to the next whenever Moscow blew the whistle. Even the stench of the Stalin-Hitler pact could not deter the core group of his learning-disabled followers, many of them Jews at that, although the chief threat they posed was to each other; they loved to stage miniature Moscow trials and quivered with delusions of power every time they could expel a fellow member for Trotskyite deviationism. As for the Marxist brothers' efforts to subvert the entertainment industry, their witless shenanigans were probably funnier than any Hollywood comedy concocted by their intended victims; how do you wash the brains of people notorious for not having any? Not funny at all, of course, were the strictly undercover activities handled by pros careful to keep out of Thirteenth Street headquarters and out of the party altogether—espionage, terror, and the infiltration of labor unions, although even those never justified the hysteria whipped up by the likes of J. Edgar Hoover and Senator McCarthy for their own nefarious purposes.

None of this surprised me. The last thing, however, I would have expected to come upon in the capital of capitalism was a vocal community of left-wing intellectuals who had openly turned against Stalin but remained committed to socialism and who now, with varying degrees of enthusiasm, supported Leon Trotsky as a plausible alternative.

I was no doubt far more impressed with this unruly crowd of dissident would-be Bolshevists and their fellow travelers than they deserved, but this, all things considered, was one error of judgment for which even I find it in my heart to forgive myself. What mostly kept the Trotskyites honest was their lack of power. But while their membership probably never topped two thousand, their influence among New York intellectuals during the 1930s was disproportionate to their numbers, though it primarily derived from the intellectual authority and stature of Leon Trotsky himself. The fact remains that they were among the first to denounce the Stalinist terror and the farce of the Moscow show trials, and that they were able to mobilize liberal and left-wing opinion in New York to an extent inconceivable at the time in Europe generally and in Belgrade in particular.

Like most sects, the Trotskyites, themselves a chip off the old Communist block, kept splintering time and again in fights over the possession and inheritance of ultimate truth, but what at that particular time went under the name of Socialist Workers Party was led by James P. Cannon, an authentic old Wobbly from Kansas, and by Max Shachtman, an equally authentic New York Jewish autodidact born in Warsaw. Their spiritual leaders included philosophy professors James Burnham, George Novak and Sidney Hook, they had an impressive following among the literary avant-garde clustered around the *Partisan Review*— Philip Rahv, Mary McCarthy, Dwight Macdonald, Edmund Wilson, Meyer Schapiro, Clement Greenberg, James Farrell among many others—and they did have a workers contingent as well, notably a group of rebellious teamsters out in Minneapolis who, by Marxist standards, qualified as proletarians. What they did not have, however, was someone who knew how to set type and operate a linotype machine.

If, like Dushan Popovich of the *Serbian Daily*, the editor of the Trotskyist weekly also ascribed my arrival on the scene to divine guidance, he did not say so.

The editor was Felix Morrow, the newspaper was the weekly *Militant*, and in his later reincarnation Felix sought guidance from oracles—Esalen, Gestalt, New Wave—that to an unrepentant atheist might seem even more dubious than the old-fashioned divinities. As an undergraduate at Columbia in the mid-1920s—where, for the sake of blending into the landscape, he changed his name from Mayerwitz—Morrow was part of a gang that included Lionel Trilling, Meyer Schapiro, Louis Hacker, Herbert Solow and others, Jewish troublemakers with a reputation for wayward brilliance who under Nicholas "Miraculous" Butler's befuddled gaze staked out a turf of their own defined by an as yet undifferentiated intellectual radicalism. Initially fellow traveling with the Communists, they publicly broke with the party as early as 1934; by 1936, when the *Partisan Review* was resurrected as a more or less Trotskyist organ, many of them had joined the left opposition. James Burnham became editor of the in principle monthly—depending on the state of the treasury—*New International*, while Felix Morrow took over the weekly *Militant*.

We had our first talk late one Sunday morning in his Greenwich Village apartment, and although both time and place had been chosen by him, he took so long answering the bell that I was about to leave when he finally opened the door. He was a sight to behold, a cross between a pajama-clad cherub and a

low-slung bulldog, bleary-eyed and disheveled, staring at me
with a noiseless growl and ready to bark, bite, or do whatever it
took to make me go away. He was some fifteen years older than
I, in his midthirties, and from where I now sit I have a great
deal of sympathy for anyone disinclined to tangle with zealous
child radicals on a Sunday morning, but at the time I was still
vigorous enough to be scandalized by such self-indulgence on
the part of a purported revolutionary, especially after he disappeared into the bathroom and kept me waiting for another
twenty minutes. Decades later I came to know the postprison
Felix as a near-respectable suburbanite with a penchant for
mysticism, mystification and space shoes, but somehow his
reformed self-image failed to convince; the puckish bulldog of
our long-ago first meeting always stubbornly superimposed
itself upon the businessman-commuter even while he, in turn,
made every effort not only to forget but to obliterate that entire
slice of his life.

What he wanted from me that Sunday morning, however,
was relatively straightforward as those things went in the naturally convoluted world of radical politics. Both the Communists
and the Trotskyists had their own print shops, unionized as a
matter of course and of principle. But whereas the printers in
the Communist shop were members of both the party and the
union, hence obliged to kick back most of their very substantial
wages, the pressman and typesetter for the Trotskyists were
ordinary middle-class proletarians who owed no allegiance to
the party and expected not only to be paid at generous union
scales, but to be paid on time, which put inordinate pressure
on the perennially depleted party coffers. The Big Six—Local 6
of the Typographical Union, AFL—was one of the most exclusive clubs in the city, virtually impossible to join without influ-
ential family connections, and even then only after a wait of
often many years. Felix halfheartedly promised nonetheless to

try and get me a union card, but in the meantime he wanted me to work in the shop on weekends and at off-hours, whenever the regular crew was not around.

Thus did I do my bit for the Revolution.

What I most enjoyed about it were, I think, the crazy hours. The two union men left at five, and we'd wander in about an hour later, Alex and I, work till two or three in the morning, then spend an hour cleaning up, putting the place back in shape just exactly as we had found it, and head home for a few hours of sleep. My partner Alex, half Irish, half Sioux—though nothing he said, especially about himself, could ever be taken seriously—was the pressman, actually a jack-of-all-trades and master of none, unless the mastery of Anglo-Saxon obscenities counts as a specialized skill; his press work stank, but his explosive reaction to a jammed roller or ink streaks on the page gave me a solid grounding in the vernacular that later came in handy in the army and has been helpful ever since. The fact that English curses suffer from a certain bloodless monotony and lack of foulminded imagination compared to Serbo-Croatian could not be held against him personally. He did the best he could, and at his best he could be damn funny.

We printed leaflets and pamphlets, including a regular German news bulletin on special tissue-thin stock, which anti-Nazi sailors smuggled into Germany; there were quite a few antifascists of various stripes among the crews of the German transatlantic liners. When those contacts were severed after the outbreak of the war and the occupation of France, we put out a French version of the bulletin. Whether any of this material ever found its way into Nazi-occupied Europe I don't know. And whether, if it did, the contents warranted jeopardizing the lives of the people involved in the distribution is one of those ultimately unanswerable questions that haunt every resistance movement.

•   •   •

I bought my first typewriter, one of those armor-plated Underwood portables made for eternity rather than disposable consumers, in a Bowery pawnshop remarkably similar to all the pawnshops along Belgrade's Balkan Street, where over the years I had hocked most of the contents of our household. Ten dollars was a fair enough price, forty galleys worth of hot scoops out of *The New York Times* freely translated by me into Serbian and simultaneously set in twelve-point Cyrillic type, though it took the threat of a strike on my part finally to get a few dollars out of crafty old Popovich. It wasn't till I was halfway out the door that he took off his battered felt hat and fished a ten-dollar bill out of the lining. "You're going to be the death of me one of these days . . ."

I have since bought many typewriters. New ones. Electric ones. Word processors, computers. I was excited, like most people, about our first car, hi-fi or television. But nothing could compare to the sense of exhilaration and of triumph with which, on a steamy August evening of my first summer in New York, I dragged that secondhand Underwood home on the subway. Those other objects were appliances, conveniences, amenities, nice to have but easy enough to do without. The Underwood was part of who I was or at least wanted to be, a statement of purpose, an affirmation of identity as well as an ever-present nagging reminder and reproach. You want to be a writer? So why the hell don't you sit down and write?

I did sit down, all right, and even did my share of typing. But self-awareness is a subtle poison, and a few drops of it in my system, just enough to realize that I was producing garbage but not enough to figure out what to do about it, effectively paralyzed the organs of inspiration. My main problem, as I saw it—like most people, I had a rather distorted view of my problems and the order of their importance—was an insufficient mastery of the English language, true enough as far as it went, but far from being the main problem. My English, quite fluent when I arrived, had been rapidly improving, and I worked at it with the sustained frenzy of an addict; the ninty-five-cent Webster's dictionary on sale at a Schulte cigar store went with me everywhere. Having already once been through the process, I was keenly aware of the difference between picking up a language and having an ongoing affair with it. Pickups are good enough for the small change of everyday intercourse and an occasional one-night stand, but the intimate relationship between writers and their medium involves passion, commitment and eternal doubt. English has never lost the allure of uncharted depths, and their exploration continues to be a challenge.

A challenge is one thing, a problem quite another. When it came to problems, the one that really tripped me up was, of course, the one I stubbornly refused to see—a visceral mistrust of authority. To ascribe it to an unresolved oedipal conflict is two-bit Freud, neither helpful nor relevant. Even as a very small child—the latency period, no less, if you believe the *Herr Professor*—most grown-ups struck me as dim-witted, crude and devoid of imagination, an opinion I saw no reason to change during my teens and which I don't think I ever quite shed. On the one hand, it spared me the heartbreak that goes with the smell of clay feet, the discovery that heroes, mentors, mother figures and surrogate fathers are human like the rest of us, and often quite a bit less so. On the other hand, it made me waste much time and energy in reinventing the wheel. All by myself. This was why for a long time I refused to entertain any notion of going back to school.

Well-meant suggestions and meddlesome advice to that effect came at me from all sides; after my pseudonymous literary debut in *The Militant* with a piece on Yugoslavia even Felix Morrow felt impelled to talk to me about college, whether by way of an oblique editorial comment or simply because he was struck by the newcomer's ignorance and naiveté I so manfully strove to dissimulate. There was, in fact, no other place in the world at that time where one could obtain a first-rate college education at practically no cost in the evening while holding down a full-time job during the day. It sounded utopian, vaguely socialist, and wholly improbable. Nevertheless, no way was I going to sit through years of boring lectures by self-important pomposities or waste chunks of my life on tests and assignments. Real learning, I believed, was strictly a do-it-yourself project. Which it is.

What in the end made me change my mind about school were a number of practical considerations, the most persuasive being a girl who attended the evening session at New York's City College and whom I rarely got to see during the week because she was too busy with her classes. A very tentative attempt to register turned out to be the fatal first step down a slippery slope. The ease with which I was admitted as a freshman despite the lack of any documents attesting to my previous schooling seemed almost shocking in its informality compared to the bureaucratic rigidity endemic in Europe; it was simply assumed that I had completed a European *Gymnasium*, and I thought it impolite to correct that assumption. The next shock was the classroom itself, the easy give-and-take between teachers and students, so vastly different from the adversarial system I had been used to. I may not have admitted it to myself at the time, but the two years I still managed to pack in at City College while waiting for Godot—or someone who looked just like him—were a learning experience in ways far beyond the mere academic. It involved the revelation that there are teachers who can actually teach, who are willing to help if one lets them, and whose help can save a great deal of time—which, as we were all subacutely aware, was rapidly running out on us. An even more intriguing discovery was the weird, orderly chaos of student politics, with Stalinists, Trotskyites, Socialists and assorted other marginal freaks, heretics and apprentice demagogues occupying separate but equal alcoves along the corridors of this pseudo-cathedral of higher learning and carrying on talmudic disputes at the top of their lungs without ever actually resorting to violence. Nothing in my previous lives had prepared me for even uncivilized shouting matches, let alone the occasional rational debates between political antagonists. In Berlin or Belgrade you didn't argue with your enemies; you hit them.

Not much has changed. Purely political differences as such are still among the least important causes of violence in this otherwise violent country, while calm and reasoned debate remains rare in Berlin and has ceased altogether in Belgrade.

Still, the reputation of New York's municipal colleges as hotbeds of radicalism seems grossly exaggerated. The amount of noise, hot air, pamphlets and polemics produced by the various sectarians gave them a visibility—and audibility—quite out of proportion to their actual numbers, and though their influence undoubtedly extended beyond the inner circle of their disciples, the vast majority of students were as indifferent to politics then as now. Yet by the end of 1939 even those whose concerns focused exclusively on Numero Uno and whose most abiding passions were played out on Ebbets Field or Yankee Stadium must have had some uneasy moments as the future—that Norman Rockwell vision of a car in every garage, a Debbie Reynolds in every bed, and 2.5 blond, freckle-faced children in every nursery—began to slip out from under them. Was there, in fact, a future in their future?

FIFTEEN

It wasn't peace that ended the First World War but mere all-around exhaustion, leading to a temporary suspension of hostilities. The break lasted a bit more than two decades; by 1939 a new crop had replaced the tired and the dead. Even in the U.S. the draft—*Selective*, no less, Service—had been reinstated, and a resumption of the interrupted slaughter was clearly imminent, investing life, at least for those of my generation still at the edge of it, with an unreal, improvisational quality that made any long-range planning seem absurd. Instead, we built castles in the sand and scanned the darkening horizon, waiting for the storm to break and the tides to carry us out to wherever.

In dreams begin responsibilities, according to Delmore Schwartz, prophet of paranoia and compulsive bottler of the *Zeitgeist*. Iridescent bubbles spawning black snakes. Waiting, we did our best to steer clear of both the bubbles and the snakes while making the most of what space remained—a twilight zone with no tomorrow that foreshadowed the intensity, exuberance and desperation of life in wartime.

The 1938 World's Fair in New York was our playground, opium for the masses, cotton candy for the intellectuals, kitsch raised to the level of pure magic, and ending on an unplanned note of nostalgia. Billed as a glimpse of the future, it turned out to have been one final backward glance at the industrial age and at the illusion of progress. A year later, as the Nazi armies swept across Europe, the lights went out on Flushing Meadows in one pavilion after another, a fitting tribute to the onset of the nuclear age.

On August 20, 1940, Leon Trotsky was killed in Mexico City by a GPU assassin.

He was sixty-one years old, one of the most brilliant demagogues of his time, father of the Red Army and "a father to many of us," as Dwight Macdonald, not given to hero worship, put it in his eulogy. Trotsky epitomized the intellectual as the man of action, hence his special appeal to frustrated American college professors who themselves always dreamed of playing ball or politics in the major leagues. He was also—though Lev Davidovich Bronstein would have been the last to acknowledge it—the Wandering Jew par excellence, hunted, haunted, shunted from Russia to Turkey to France to Norway to Mexico in the futile quest for a refuge from probably the closest thing to evil incarnate that ever walked the earth. In the long run, nothing and no one could have saved him from Stalin's army of thugs; neither the fortified villa in Coyoacan nor the fresh-faced, pistol-packing American youngsters who mounted guard around the clock but never thought of stopping the urbane Spaniard who carried a pickax under his raincoat.

Politically, of course, Trotsky had been dead ever since Lenin's funeral, which he was too depressed to attend. And all his dialectical sophistry notwithstanding, the brutal Georgian psychopath was a decidedly far more plausible heir to Lenin than a neurotic Jewish intellectual. But he kept up the fight because he was a fighter, hard though it seems to believe that so astute a political observer could really have fooled himself about the odds; his Fourth International was a farce, and his chances of replacing Stalin about as great as Czar Nicholas's chances of rising from the dead. And yet his murder was a major blow to the anti-Stalinist left. Not only did it silence a powerful voice, but it also demonstrated the ruthless efficiency of Stalin's global terror network. Its hit men had now successfully eliminated all of Trotsky's family, with the exception of his wife and single surviving grandson, who was spirited away and secretly raised in Mexico under an assumed name.

Today he lives quietly and openly in Coyoacan in what is left of the fortress on the Avenida Vienna, tending the garden where the ashes of his grandparents are buried and guiding visitors—predominantly Russians—through Leon Trotsky's last sanctuary.

A final footnote to the history of the Russian Revolution.

Trotskyism in America briefly survived the death of the leader. The Nazi invasion of Russia in the summer of 1941 exacerbated tensions within the party between the followers of James Cannon, who saw Russian socialism as degenerate but still worth defending, and the partisans of Max Schachtman, to whom the Soviet Union had become just another totalitarian regime. The theological dispute, carried on with a solemn ferocity as though Russia's future hinged on the outcome, finally led to an open break, with each faction claiming the mantle of the martyred leader. In the meantime Roosevelt paid off a political debt to Daniel J. Tobin, head of the AFL, by—at the very least—sanctioning the indictment of twenty-nine leading Trotskyites, including most specifically the dissident Minneapolis teamsters who had committed the potentially precedent-setting crime of leaving the AFL and leading their members into the CIO instead. Eighteen of the party's leaders, James Cannon and Felix Morrow among them, were eventually convicted under the

Smith Act of advocating the overthrow of the government by force and went to prison for terms ranging from twelve to sixteen months. The trial and verdict generated remarkably little protest in liberal and leftist circles busy by then rooting for embattled Russia and her avuncular leader, and the Communists, having switched overnight from militant pacifism to even more militant patriotism, were fulsome in their support of the Smith Act. Which made it rather difficult to sympathize with the plight of their own leaders when, after the war, they in turn were sentenced under the same law to substantial prison terms.

After the death of the Old Man, as they characteristically referred to him among themselves, many of his fatherless children became *enfants terribles* of a different sort. Some adopted Mao or Lyndon Larouche, others turned to god, money and the flag in the hour of their need. James Burnham conducted a one-man managerial revolution in Henry Luce's *Fortune*, Max Schachtman preached a radical brand of superpatriotism, Irving Kristol brokered marriages between Jewish reactionaries and right-wing anti-Semites, Felix Morrow dabbled in publishing, mysticism and Esalen. Most just quietly scattered and disappeared, swallowed up by the war, the army, or simple indifference.

Long before the assassination I had in fact begun to doubt that true socialism as I understood it—and still understand it— was compatible with any kind of dictatorship, be it in the name of Stalin, Trotsky, or the faceless proletariat. The inane factional squabbles characterized by a conspicuous absence of even the most common sense, let alone a sense of humor or proportion, further reinforced my misgivings. Since doubt equals heresy among the vanguard of the revolution, I would have faced ceremonial expulsion had I not simply faded away, like so many of the party's stars.

What partly accounted for my gradual withdrawal from the outer fringes of futility may have been a growing awareness of both self and of the American experience, but major credit undoubtedly goes to Ruth. We met at that rather critical juncture in both our lives, and from the very first she provided a sturdy link to the real world that has sustained me now for over half a century.

As a resident alien I became eligible for the draft in January of 1941, on my twenty-first birthday. Under the complicated lottery system in force at the time, each draft board was assigned a quota, the rate of the call-up depending on the number of qualified bodies available in any particular district in any given month. In practice this meant having to put one's life on hold, often for many months, in anticipation of personal greetings from the President of the United States.

Although the war in Europe was already into its second year, America remained almost defiantly at peace in the summer of '41. At peace, and at work; the push to bolster U.S. defenses while at the same time meeting the increasingly desperate needs of both the British and the Russians had at long last all but eliminated unemployment. But there was something palpably spurious and artificial about the disquieting calm and the sudden prosperity, and even the euphoria that goes with being in love could not quite make us ignore the futility of any long-range plans for the future. Some day we might have a life together, but the *some day* hung in the distant sky like a mirage. What loomed immediately ahead was separation and the uncertainty beyond.

Still, we had the summer together, thanks to the surfeit of sturdy, milk-fed twenty-one-year-olds in the West Bronx, which delayed my induction from month to month until finally in late November I received my preliminary notice. Two weeks later, on December 7, the Japanese bombed Pearl Harbor, the U.S. declared war on Germany and Japan, and as a German-born noncitizen, my status changed overnight from prospective defender of democracy to Enemy Alien.

Compared to the way the Japanese—citizens and noncitizens alike—were dealt with on the West Coast, the treatment of German-born aliens was exceedingly benign; we were forbidden to own shortwave equipment and had to notify the FBI every time we traveled more than one hundred miles beyond our official residence, measures that made no conceivable sense but presumably kept a fair number of bureaucrats happily occupied. For me personally it meant another surcease; no enemy aliens would be drafted until U.S. authorities had a chance to review the individual cases and separate the Nazis from the anti-Nazis. And though they moved with quite remarkable dispatch, they made us a gift of one more winter and half a summer; it was not until August of 1942 that I finally reported to Fort Dix, New Jersey, for induction.

CHAPTER

SIXTEEN

The mobilization of eleven million American civilians in World War II was a case of the blind leading the blind; all the more reason to regard it in retrospect as a rare triumph of improvisation and adaptability. There were no precedents. The brief and limited U.S. engagement in the First World War offered few valid guidelines, and the cadres of the peacetime regular army, a scruffy lot of drunks, drifters and derelicts suddenly propelled into a leadership status for which they were in no way prepared, merely contributed further to the massive initial confusion. Under the circumstances, the fact that millions of men were actually drafted, equipped, housed, fed, trained, assigned and eventually shipped to the far corners of the earth looms as an impressive tribute to the spirit of collective enterprise and to the managerial skills of American industry.

That the process was flawed and enormously wasteful is no secret; everyone who ever served in the army can testify to monumental foul-ups, and the antic idiocies of life in uniform formed the basis for a whole subspecies of popular entertainment. But that was to be expected; shocking is not how much went wrong but how much went right, given the odds. The sleepy, dim-witted corporal who administered and scored IQ tests at two o'clock in the morning during the initial round-the-clock processing at Fort Dix, or the classification clerks who, with no background in personnel work whatsoever, interviewed hundreds of recruits each day and fed the questionable results into IBM punchcards created obvious bottlenecks; the IQ tests ultimately proved as worthless as the punchcards. But incompetence, inexperience and sheer stupidity persisted at higher and highest levels, often producing results that were anything but funny.

None of which really mattered in the end. Wanton waste is as American as apple pie and assault rifles, and the army wasted manpower and resources with truly prodigious abandon. The point is, we could afford to; that was how we won the war. As they said—and still go on saying—there is always more where that came from. The thought that some day soon this may cease to be true goes against the American grain.

We won the war. Won it not with a whimper but a bang— this, too, thanks to America's ability and willingness to waste vast resources on a very dubious project, and to the—albeit selective—hospitality generously extended to a group of anti-Nazi refugees. It is easy, with hindsight, to question the wisdom of Einstein, Fermi, Lise Meitner, Szilard, Teller, von Neumann et al in spawning a Golem that threatens mankind with extinction. At the time it was Hitler who loomed as the larger and far more imminent threat.

The stated purpose of Basic Training is to turn civilians into soldiers. This involves a regression to childhood which many people find exhilarating. I certainly did. Marching through

Georgia in mid-August with full gear may not be everyone's idea of fun, but it beat indoor work, especially the kind I'd been wasting my life on for years. There was an abundance of toys to play with—rifles, machine guns, bayonets, grenades, explosives, everything I'd ever fantasized about as a kid, and to paraphrase Freud's remark about his cigar just being a cigar, sometimes a rifle is merely a long tube subject to frequent inspections, just like the organ it is said to symbolize. The loss of individual rights is offset by freedom from individual responsibility, a trade-off that must be counted among the major attractions of army life. Boredom, on the other hand, a particularly virulent strain of corrosive inanition rampant among the military, happened to be one scourge to which by a stroke of good fortune, weird genes or simplemindedness I turned out to be immune. Having to live in close quarters and in unremitting intimacy with dozens, sometimes hundreds of men—white men, I should qualify—from all over the country and from every social stratum can make angels drop their halos; what it did to me was confront me with my ignorance and my pretensions. It forced me to see how little I knew about people, how little I knew about America, and how much even what little I did know was mere pallid theory filtered through academic abstraction.

I had read Faulkner and was reasonably up on the history of the labor movement, but I had never met people like Brumbalow and Kowalski in the flesh. They had the bunks on either side of me. Brumbalow, a farm boy from near Tupelo, Mississippi, could lift a jeep with his bare hands but wasn't used to wearing shoes, and even with his size thirteen special issue he used to regularly collapse after trudging along for a mile or two, stretch out by the roadside and call for the loo-tenant to shoot him. "Tha's what they do to horses, ain't it?" He had never even been as far as Jackson, and the only book he'd ever cracked was a Dick and Jane reader, which left him with a permanent, well-founded distaste for printed matter. His snoring shook the rafters and took some getting used to, but he had a sweet temper when he was sober, which somewhat made up for the noise and which, with my lingering Tolstoyan romanticism, I misread for the basic goodness of man rooted in the soil until one night he rolled in drunk, roused me out of my sleep, demanded to know why the fuck I was always reading fucking books, threatened to beat the shit out of me and would no doubt have done so had he been able to catch me as he stumbled about in the dark barracks. We ended up, half a dozen of us, dumping him into the shower, clothes and all, and by next morning he was his meek old self again. But he taught me that while happy families may be all alike, when it comes to Mississippi farmers, trust Faulkner rather than Tolstoy.

Brumbalow never shipped out with us. Ever easygoing, he erupted in the orderly room one day, damn near killed the first sergeant and presumably spent the rest of the war in the pen, which at the very least kept him safe if not sound. My neighbor to the right, Mike Kowalski from Aliquippa, Pennsylvania, was not nearly as lucky. The son and grandson of coal miners, he was an almost androgynously graceful youngster, undereducated but with a searching mind and an insatiable curiosity, the only one in the company interested in my own receding past and in the events that led up to the war. Happy to have kept out of the mines, he was eager to go overseas and see the world, or as much of it as the army would let him, and determined, if he liked what he saw, not ever to go back to Aliquippa.

He never did. Curiosity made him try to dismantle a German hand grenade he picked up along the road in Tunisia shortly after we landed. He was our first casualty.

Fifty years ago, in the days before television and air travel shrank the country and the world, regional and cultural differences among people from diverse parts of the U.S. were vastly more pronounced than they are now. Of the millions of draftees sluiced through these southern camps, the overwhelming majority came from somewhere east of the Rockies and had never traveled more than a few hundred miles beyond their home base. And while the Hollywood cliché of the brotherhood of arms among soldiers of disparate creed, class or ethnic origin— so long as it was more or less white—reeked of sanctimony and propaganda, the actual degree of tolerance among randomly assembled groups of inveterate civilians forced to live in close quarters and act like soldiers seemed to me rather remarkable at the time. It still does. There were strict limits to it, and it varied enormously among camps and units. But the mafioso from Brooklyn, the Tupelo farmer, the hell-and-brimstone fundamentalist from South Carolina and the insurance salesman from Minnesota got along, and they accepted me as just another nut case from New York, a guy who didn't drink and kept a fucking library in his fucking footlocker, just as they accepted David Shapiro from Brooklyn, who slipped out of bed each day at dawn to strap on phylacteries and quietly mumbled his morning prayers. David, in fact, awed them.

This although I overheard a voluble discussion among a contingent of not quite sober crackers as to whether or not a Jew was a white man. They wouldn't go quite so far as to say that he was, but then again they allowed that he wasn't black, either.

Black was, in fact, a different story altogether.

There is no way in which I or any white person, not even a Jew, could begin to know what it meant to be black in Macon, Georgia, in 1942. Nor anywhere else, either, for that matter, and a case can be made—and has been made—that in institutionalizing racism, the South was merely being less hypocritical about it than the North with its unofficial urban ghettos. Perhaps. But nothing, neither the black neighborhoods of New York and Philadelphia nor the voluminous literature on the Civil War still raging in the South had prepared me for the utter barbarity of segregation in what in a way were merely its most superficial and yet at the same time its most striking day-to-day manifestations—separate drinking fountains, toilets, lunch counters, churches, service clubs, entrances to theaters and public buildings, transportation—inescapable symbols of a fundamental assault on human dignity, a systematized dehumanization beyond anything I could have imagined and a throwback to precisely the sort of medieval mind-set that characterized the Nazis and which we were supposedly fighting against. That people's bias would not easily yield to reason soon became obvious in spirited barracks discussions with segregationists. In no way, however, did this exculpate the government, whose support of segregation in fact and in law seemed rather difficult to reconcile with its ringing affirmation of the Four Freedoms proclaimed as major war aims. And while governments the world over engage in hypocrisy, they generally do so quite deliberately and without fooling anyone, least of all themselves. In America, on the other hand, sanctimony has evolved into an indigenous art form, practiced by preachers, politicians, publicists and even ordinary citizens with such fervent dedication that one is sometimes tempted to think they actually believe what they are saying.

Some apparently do. But in Macon, Columbia or Augusta, not to mention the United States Army, even the pernicious, self-serving fiction of separate but equal was nowhere in evidence. Separate, definitely. Equal? No way.

Perhaps it is the sheer size of the country that accounts for the pervasive fear of loneliness, the desperate notion that almost anyone's company is preferable to coming face-to-face with one's own self. Even where there was no conceivable need for socializing, soldiers would invariably huddle in clusters spontaneously formed for whatever the occasion—going to the movies, the whorehouse, the Post Exchange, perfect strangers in quest not of warmth, friendship, intimacy so much as of protection against solitude. Social life in America revolves around the duality of bar and church; liquor and/or piety—by no means mutually exclusive—govern most collective rituals, from college reunions to politics, and from Christmas parties to philanthropy. As a consequence, people who neither drink nor worship are very much on their own, in the army as in civilian life, a fairly normal situation in my case, to which I was quite accustomed and which did not strike me as particularly problematic. In any event, there was nothing to be done about it short of learning to talk baseball and go to town with the boys on Saturday night to get drunk, laid and sick in approximately that order, none of which appealed to my fastidious socialist tastes. Yet in spite of these social handicaps I got along quite well with most of the men in my company; some were easier to talk to than others, as weird in their ways as I was in my own, though not quite weird enough to form any close friendships.

If there was one thing that struck me as more esoteric than baseball statistics, it was piety of whatever denomination, one reason why it never occurred to me to attend services in the Post chapel or to present my credentials to the Jewish chaplain. But in the end the rabbi, a vapid and presumptuous little squirt masquerading as a U.S. Army captain, managed to get even.

Two weeks into the new year, in January 1943, the regiment and in fact almost the entire camp were put on the alert for shipment overseas. All furloughs were canceled, so that our plans for a spring wedding in New York went down the drain and it became clear that if we were still going to get married before I shipped out, it would have to be in Georgia. And soon.

Ruth was willing to do her share by coming down from Philadelphia, a minimally twenty-four-hour trip on badly over-crowded wartime trains, while it was up to me to settle the technicalities. Judging from the epidemic of wartime marriages and the emotional wreckage left in their wake, getting married was, if anything, far too easy. Any idiot could, and did, do it, the Army's sixty-dollar monthly family allowance providing a pow-erful incentive for casual couplings. Justices of the Peace were sprouting like alfalfa all along the Georgia–South Carolina state line, performing weddings around the clock at five bucks a throw, and thousands of homesick, lonely GIs got hitched on the spur of the moment to women they barely knew but who looked pretty good to them at two in the morning by the light of a forty-watt bulb. It did not seem a very appetizing way to legitimize our relationship, and with some reluctance I turned to the Jewish USO for advice on alternatives.

The acronym stood, or stands, for United Service Organiza-tions. Feeble irony or feebleminded hypocrisy, because far from being united, these service clubs were segregated according to both denomination and color, one each for white Protestants, Catholics and Jews, and one for blacks of whatever faith. But for once I was in luck; the Jewish USO was being run by one of those fairy godmothers one reads about but seldom meets up with in real life, a woman who quite simply offered to take charge of everything. One condition: "That you let me buy you a steak dinner after the wedding."

Small, birdlike but imperious, Esther had been a Park Avenue socialite in an earlier life, a member of the German-Jewish aris-tocracy, before the war took her son, an Air Force pilot killed on a training flight. Grief galvanized her into action; she sought refuge in work, in Dixie, in mothering people her child's age, all of which she did with relentless dedication and the utmost competence without ever allowing the hurt to show. When it turned out that I would not be able to get a pass on my wedding day— marriage was not nearly as big a deal as the infiltration course— she waved her magic wand and arranged to have the blood test waived and the city registry reopened in the evening. She also asked the Jewish chaplain to make himself available for a late night ceremony at the USO, a pointed request which in view of his military status he was in no position to refuse, much as he no doubt would have liked to. By failing to attend his services and play sheep to his shepherd I had placed myself beyond the pale, as far as he was concerned, but it was his vanity that pinched this self-important vessel of divine wisdom most of all, to the point where he snidely announced that as an Orthodox rabbi he would only officiate at an Orthodox wedding.

What Orthodox Judaism has going for it, in my book, is that it makes no pretense at spreading sweetness, light or—god forbid—love. It offers no apologies for the intolerance, the narrow-minded bias and the contempt for outsiders it shares with all other orthodoxies, most of which, however, carry on about loving their neighbors even while they burn and slaughter them for the good of their souls. The rabbi made it plain that he had no use for us, and I was about ready to ignore his captain's bars and let him know what I thought of him or at the very least to walk out and head for the nearest Justice of the Peace. But by then it was close to midnight, I had to be back in camp by 5 A.M., and in the end common sense, or rather Ruth, prevailed, as she has since on countless similar occasions, and that was how we got married in the Jewish USO by an Orthodox rabbi, although the ritual purity of the ceremony seemed seriously compromised by the musical schmaltz which a lady piano player, borrowed for the occasion from the Protestant USO, was unwisely prevailed upon to provide.

A week later I was on a troop ship, bound for North Africa.

SEVENTEEN

The barren hills on the outskirts of the city had been turned into one vast staging area, with thousands upon thousands of men, vehicles and equipment littering the hillsides in patterns not apparent to the ant's eye view. There was no escape from the African sun, but Lyster bags full of near-boiling, heavily chlorinated water hung suspended from tripods like bloated cows' udders, and the latrines—a breezy open-air arrangement of poles over lime-filled ditches improvised to cope with a mass outbreak of diarrhea—afforded a majestic view of the Mediterranean as long as one managed to maintain one's balance on the perch. The view was even more breathtaking at night, with a total blackout in effect and the cloudless African sky opening out onto the universe.

Oran itself, roughly a thousand years old, intermittently Moorish, Spanish, Turkish, French and marked by all its conquerors for better and for worse, did not seem like much of a place to these transient hordes from across the sea who missed the familiar landmarks—Main Street, Woolworth, the clapboard church, the lunch counter, gas station and county courthouse—that in their mind's eye defined a town as such. But Oran held two major tourist attractions for the GI just disembarked after an abstemious two-week sea voyage and living on C rations in the sunbaked hills above the city: black market restaurants and a monumental four-story whorehouse.

The restaurants served miserable food at exorbitant prices, but even the leathery backside of a senile camel made for a gourmet meal after a steady diet of six cans of cold cat food a day. And price simply didn't matter. With an indifference to basic economics that bordered on criminal stupidity, the U.S. government allowed its soldiers overseas to collect their full pay in cash. Since even an American buck private made five times as much as his British counterpart, ten times as much as a French soldier, and more in a month than most natives earned in a year, prices after the American landing exploded with the violence and abruptness of a string of land mines. A bottle of wine went from ten francs to one hundred fifty and way beyond; most GIs didn't really care how much of this toy money they threw away, thus effectively pricing our allies out of the competition for booze and sex. Not surprisingly, the allies in turn failed to appreciate our generous support of indigenous pimps and black marketeers, which gave rise to a certain amount of anti-American sentiment.

The mass appeal of the whorehouse, on the other hand, was somewhat more difficult to fathom, even if one lacked the moral and esthetic sensibility of an Eleanor Roosevelt, said to have been instrumental in finally closing down the place. The French had maintained a standing army in the region since the days of Napoleon, along with the naval base at Mers-el-Kébir in the Oran harbor and the headquarters of the Foreign Legion at nearby Sidi-bel-Abbès. And being French, hence unjudgmentally practical about sex, they had built a four-story military brothel and staffed it with another kind of foreign legion, this one consisting of women from all over the at the time still far-flung empire, designed to meet the sexual needs of their sometimes fighting men while at the same time minimizing the spread of venereal diseases through strict on-the-spot sanitary controls.

It was an efficient supermarket type of operation that had far more in common with pay toilets than with sex. There were obligatory condoms and chits good for a ten-minute love-in on sale at the entrance, and a prophylactic station by way of a checkout administering stinging preventive treatment to each patron as he left. When they first came upon it right after the initial landings, the American top brass popped their buttons with sheepish admiration. It must have struck them as an inspired solution to a vexing problem, and one wholly consistent with the entrepreneurial philosophy that was part of our mission to the world.

In front of the shit-colored brick building guarded by white-helmeted MPs, hundreds of GIs sweated out long lines every day, braving the murderous sun and patiently waiting their turn at what, after hours of eager anticipation, was generally reviled as a horrendous letdown compared to the whorehouses back home, about as erotically gratifying an experience as being dragged naked through a car wash. And still they came with each new convoy, horny, curious and scared, many more of them virgins than would freely admit it, until moral outrage prevailed in Washington and the brothel was ordered closed. Sanctimony, thy name is Congress. Pursuant to the ukase, our clean-cut American boys henceforth stopped patronizing prostitutes and kept themselves pure for their very own little women chastely pining away for them back in the good old U.S.A. And they lived happily ever after.

•   •   •

By the time we left the staging area and headed east toward Tunisia, most of North Africa had been cleared of Germans. *Liberated*, of course, was the operative word commonly used by us liberators, but as I was soon to find out, the Arabs as well as the French attached their own different and diametrically opposite interpretations to that word. The week-long trek along the spine of the mountain chain that closely hugs the coastline of Algeria was itself a strangely liberating experience, even though bouncing around eight hours a day in a two-and-a-half-ton truck without springs can be hard on the kidneys. The roads were rutted but spectacular, with abrupt transitions from barren rocks with stunning vistas of the sea to sudden dips into dark forests and long stretches of dusty trails through war-battered villages, with Arab kids lining the roadsides screaming for chewing gum and selling bottles of a yellow liquid which, by the time the hapless GI uncorked it a few miles further down the road, turned out to be something other than wine. The steady movement through an ever-changing landscape, the nightly bivouacs under the open skies and the quiet demise of the chickenshit spit and polish that goes with stateside soldiering conveyed a bracing if short-lived illusion of peacetime adventure.

The vagabondage ended at Mateur, a small town in eastern Tunisia which, though it had suffered extensive damage in the fighting, was still inhabited and served as advance headquarters of the Allied command. We pitched our tents at the outskirts, pending further orders; aside from being attached to the Quartermaster Corps, the precise purpose and function of our company still remained a closely guarded secret while in the meantime the Spirit of the Pioneers and of the Old West asserted itself and, within days, transformed the campsite into a rudimentary village. Foraging parties combed the hillsides scrounging for wood and scrap lumber, the pup tents acquired walls

cobbled together out of packing crates, rough picnic tables and
benches appeared throughout the campsite, a nearby laundry
unit provided hot showers, a Kentucky barber set up an out-
door shop, and the kitchen began to supplement the regular GI
rations with poultry, fruit and vegetables bartered from Arab
farmers against cigarettes and other basic luxuries. Being the
only French speaker around, I found myself constantly dragged
into these transactions, but while I did not mind so much dealing with the Arabs, things got sticky when my linguistic talents
came to the attention of a group of French officers encamped
in the vicinity with their Senegalese troops. They zeroed in on
us like a swarm of mosquitoes, and the shameless greed with
which they begged, grabbed and demanded cigarettes and just
about everything else within sight would have embarrassed
most natives. Yet at the same time they knew how to season
their arrogance with a hefty portion of Gallic charm, not quite
enough to mask their utter contempt for Americans but sufficient to butter up our own none too swift officers in spite of the
language barrier. Their ambitions extended way beyond retail
schnorring into wholesale black-marketeering, but being merely
professional soldiers, they lacked the guts, the subtlety and
brains of true gangsters. Their efforts to recruit me as a potential
accomplice by faking friendship were merely pathetic, until the
night they warned me against any dealings with Jews, and most
particularly against entanglements with Jewish women. "They
are very beautiful and very dangerous." I never saw the bastards
again.

The warning came too late, in any case; by that time I was
already deeply involved with a number of Jewish women other
than my wife, most of them ranging in age from about four to
ten.

The day after our arrival I walked into Mateur and discovered that the place, though devastated and largely in ruins, was still inhabited, and that inexplicably most of the inhabitants seemed to be destitute, Arab-speaking Jews. It was difficult to make contact until—appropriately enough amidst the wreckage of what had been the town's one-room public library—I met Gigitte.

Like myself she was scrounging among the few undamaged books, a totally improbable apparition with her freckled face and her shock of red hair, all of eight years old but more poised and articulate than most teenagers I'd ever known. Her formal name, as she gravely informed me, was Huguette, but everyone called her Gigitte. She had an older sister named Suzanne, and they lived with their grandparents, because their parents were dead.

The child was irresistible, spontaneous and self-possessed, full of mischief yet at the same time wise way beyond her years, with the sort of wisdom that the need to survive against the odds will occasionally instill in even the very young. Beyond that she was quite simply very bright; though she spoke only Arabic at home, she was also fluent in French and loved to read books, which she had not been able to do ever since Jewish children were banned from school the previous year.

It was love at first sight, a veritable *coup de foudre*, and there was a time when, in my blissful ignorance of what parenting was all about, I quite seriously thought of adopting Gigitte; her grandparents would probably have raised far fewer objections than my level-headed wife. In the end the bureaucratic obstacles loomed insuperable, but she became my faithful guide and interpreter throughout the summer. Thanks to her I was able to talk to people around town, and what they told me about their experiences with the Nazis in Tunisia seemed at first blush a highly implausible story. Rommel's troops, even while fighting the Allies, had apparently not been too busy to also conduct extensive roundups of North African Jews with the help of Vichy French and pro-Nazi Arabs, and Mateur served as a sort of preliminary concentration camp. Which explained why there were only Jews in town and why they had not been able to flee during the fighting, but it raised a bigger question, one to which at the time none of us had a plausible answer: Why did the Nazis, engaged in a last-ditch struggle to maintain their foothold in Africa, divert vital resources to this insane, ideologically inspired enterprise, and what, precisely, did they ultimately intend to do with these thousands of Jews?

Failure of the imagination. Forgivable, though not quite. Someone could have told us; by the spring of '43, the Warsaw ghetto had already been liquidated.

Rommel's last stand had fizzled, Tunis had fallen, the Afrika Korps had surrendered, our campsite in the hills had turned into a regular little village, and still we were kept in the dark as to the ultimate assignment of our rather peculiar mobile company. Meanwhile we had absolutely nothing to do other than hunt down phantom Nazi parachutists reputed to have been sighted in the area by native informants expecting a handsome reward. It struck me that the Jewish children in Mateur were similarly at loose ends, having had no school for nearly a year, and rather than wasting my time playing cowboys and Indians, I obtained permission to go to town every morning and try to organize something resembling rudimentary education. Gigitte rounded up some two dozen of her friends and relatives, I liberated a supply of pencils and paper, and we claimed squatters' rights in the ruins of the schoolhouse, but that was where my troubles began.

Some of the youngest did not yet know how to read, and even many of the older ones, despite several years of prewar schooling, had forgotten much of their French. My efforts to recruit help among the adults of the community met with stubborn if not downright hostile resistance on the part of the men; they were themselves for the most part illiterate, and their attitudes toward women as well as education combined the nastiest aspects of both Jewish and Muslim fundamentalism. The women, on the other hand—or at least the few willing to risk talking to me in Gigitte's presence and out of sight of their husbands—were wildly enthusiastic about the project, several of them clearly literate enough to lend a hand, but none would volunteer, even though I myself offered to withdraw.

That left me stuck with the job, and I did the best I could. The kids themselves were a big help. By the end of the first week we had about fifty would-be pupils, with Gigitte and some of the better readers teaching the beginners while I worked with the older ones on reading, writing and the fundamentals of arithmetic. On-the-job training for teachers is probably no riskier than in most other fields, although a self-taught surgeon might be perceived as more of an immediate threat, and my performance in the improvised, roofless classroom undoubtedly flunked all professional criteria. I had, however, one enormous advantage over most professionals: the kids who came flocking to this makeshift establishment were all of them desperately eager to learn.

I did what I could to help tide them over until regular schooling resumed the following spring, long after we had left, and I hope they brought to it some of the same joy and exuberance with which they showed up every morning in the musty ruins that with the help of a little imagination and an ever-cloudless sky we transformed into a school. One thing is certain: I learned a great deal more from them than they could possibly have learned from me. But that probably happens even to real teachers.

•   •   •

After nearly four weeks of peaceful anarchy the company was made to assemble one morning in the clearing that had become a sort of village green, and our dashing captain, a crackerjack vacuum cleaner salesman from Jacksonville, Florida, finally revealed to us our collective fate and function in this war. We were to be divided into half a dozen teams which, with the aid of civilians hired locally, would run Army Post Exchanges throughout the Theater of Operations and assure a steady supply of Hershey bars and cigarettes to the GIs at and behind the front.

They also serve who only run the store.

The news was greeted with understandable enthusiasm. Some of the men were seasoned crooks from way back; a clique involving the mess sergeant and his cronies had already been stealing our meat rations back in Georgia and selling them on the black market. Everybody knew about it, nobody did anything about it—if you're a GI, you don't mess with a mess sergeant from Brooklyn, and if you are an officer, well, you close your eyes and hold out your hand, palm up. Yet even those pure of heart with only the least trace of larceny in it could not fail to realize, after a couple of months in this war-ravaged country, that supervising the distribution of vast quantities of goods wholly unavailable to civilians offered many easy ways to get rich and—more important, instant gratification being what it is—even easier ways to get laid. Cigarette power. Chewing gum power. But whatever their reactions, no one in that clearing, so far as I could tell, asked the Lord not to lead him into temptation.

In fact, I seemed to be the only one unhappy about the prospects before us. My years at Geza Kon had left me with a visceral loathing for anything having to do with shopkeeping, and I certainly couldn't see myself as manager of the military version of a trading post, balancing books and bossing a locally recruited work force, though all around me guys began salivating audibly at the mere thought of being able to hire themselves a harem. Which, as it turned out, is exactly what they did.

That very afternoon I walked into the offices of G-2, the military intelligence section of Eastern Base Headquarters in Mateur, and asked for a job.

EIGHTEEN

Had I known then what I found out a few months later, I never would have had the nerve to walk into Lt. Col. Johnson's office. Under the secret rules of the game as played back in Washington, the mere fact of asking to be assigned to Intelligence automatically marked the applicant as a potential suspect and caused him to be barred from any sensitive post for the rest of his life, natural or otherwise.

Half a century of cold war, space-age technology and unlimited funds may have transformed military intelligence from a mere oxymoron into a billion-dollar boondoggle, but what few glimpses we have been vouchsafed of its operations in places like Iran, Nicaragua, Vietnam and Afghanistan suggest that it has never outgrown the zany incoherence of its spooky beginnings. The outbreak of the war caught the U.S. not only unprepared but also hopelessly uninformed, and the post-Pearl Harbor hysteria precipitated frantic efforts to create an instant intelligence service. The results were largely unfortunate and often disastrous, Lt. Col. Johnson being one of the latter.

Ruddy, hairless and rotund, rather like a small bad egg on top of a large one in appearance, Col. Johnson played by nobody's rules but his own, which he made up as he went along. The sheriff of Jerkwater County, Florida, he had been commissioned under a policy based on the army's conceit that somehow law enforcement constituted the ideal preparation both for spying and for catching spies. Put in charge of countersubversive operations at Allied Force Headquarters in Algiers, the then major had sniffed out so many Nazis and Communists in our own army that finally "some pinko bastard on Ike's staff," as he put it, got him promoted out and put in charge of eastern base intelligence, presumably on the assumption that in the boondocks he would be kept out of harm's way. It was a decision they soon came to regret. If there was one thing the colonel hated worse than Commies it was foreigners, and a large part of his new job revolved around dealing with Frogs, Jerries and Ayrabs. Ever the diplomat, he made it known that if it were up to him, he'd shoot the whole damn lot, but in the meantime he faced some practical problems not of his own making. Most specifically, several German POWs had escaped and been recaptured, other Germans claimed to be anti-Nazis and apparently tried to switch sides, and Johnson was expected to submit detailed reports on these cases to Algiers. The trouble was that no one on his staff spoke enough German to interrogate the prisoners. He may therefore, I suppose, be forgiven if he so to speak hired me on the spot without checking my credentials. Had he done so, he probably would have had me shot along with the prisoners. As is, it may have been the single most intelligent move of his entire career. Two days later I left the tent camp and moved into the ruins of a large villa in Mateur that housed the entire twenty-man staff of the G-2 Section, officers as well as enlisted men.

• • •

Prisoner interrogation.

With the surrender of Rommel's Afrika Korps, the U.S. Army found itself with some thirty thousand prisoners on its hands who—for reasons I to this day fail to understand—were to be shipped to the U.S. Pending embarkation, they were being held in improvised transit camps in Tunisia, from which a few had escaped and tried to make their way to neutral Tangier or Spanish Morocco. The French, however, had an efficient network of police and informers covering every town and village, and although escaped Nazis worried them far less than Arab nationalists, they were always eager to bag them and find out if there weren't any natives they could shoot for having helped the escapees along the way.

The three prisoners they brought in on my first day on the job were veterans of the Afrika Korps, deeply tanned, blond hair bleached to near-white, still cocky though manifestly scared, not of the colonel—let alone of me—but of the two burly Frenchmen in civilian clothes who conducted most of the interrogations, with me serving as interpreter. The prisoners readily admitted that they had intended to make their way to the coast, steal a boat and try to cross over into Sicily, but they balked at answering any questions about where they had hidden out during the six-day escapade and how they had managed to feed themselves.

The colonel, accustomed to bullying hick-town burglars and car thieves, was clearly out of his depth and merely wondered out loud why anyone would want to forgo an all-expense paid trip to god's own country. The Germans didn't deign to answer, the French failed to appreciate the humor. Although they didn't speak a word of German, they grew increasingly restless, impatient with having to go through me rather than dealing directly with their victims. They asked them if they ever expected to see their mothers again, but while I could translate the question literally, I had no way of investing my version with the menacing growl of the original. Finally, after a brief private consultation, the agents proposed to take the prisoners to a French army jail near Gabès for further interrogation, and the colonel, eager to be shut out of the whole mess, readily agreed. "Ask them if they got someone who can talk to them down there."

I asked. They laughed. "We'll talk to them all right," said the older one, briefly baring his rotten teeth. *"Par téléphone."*

By phone? I had no idea what he was talking about and simply skipped that remark. They left as glum-faced as they had arrived, though not nearly as glum as their Nazi prisoners.

A few weeks later, browsing in a Tunis bookstore, I was accosted by a young Arab who, in flawless French, expressed polite astonishment at an American GI interested in French literature and invited me to have coffee with him at a nearby sidewalk café. He identified himself as a member of the outlawed Neo-Destour party and complained that the Americans seemed unaware of the atrocities the French—the army as well as local authorities, all of them Vichy fascists, according to him—were committing against the native population in order to suppress the independence movement. They were shooting Arabs every day, some of them freedom fighters, many others totally innocent. "But you know," he said, "when they hook you up to a battery-operated field telephone, with one clamp on your prick and the other on your nose, and they start turning the crank, you'll confess to anything."

He just wanted me to know. And tell my compatriots about it. "They're good people. But ignorant."

Much more distressing: the three *Wehrmacht* sad sacks singled out as troublemakers by our MPs because they accused their fellow prisoners of wanting to kill them. They turned out to be members of the 999th Disciplinary Regiment, an outfit composed of former concentration camp inmates, political prisoners who had been given a chance to "redeem themselves" by serving in the Nazi army. Dumped at the last minute into North Africa as cannon fodder in an already lost cause, they deserted first chance they got, but instead of receiving the welcome they had expected, they found themselves herded into the same compounds as the hard-core Nazis of the Afrika Korps who, no longer having us to fight, turned on them with merciless savagery and threatened to liquidate anyone maligning the Führer.

Three gaunt, middle-aged men, trade union veterans who had spent most of the Hitlerite thirties in concentration camps, pleading with dignified passion for their own lives and those of their fellow anti-Nazis. The other Germany. The man to whom they tried to explain their ethical and political opposition to Nazism and who decided whether their plea would even be passed on up the chain of command was a dumb hick-town sheriff with a sixth-grade education to whom all fucking Germans were alike. "Let 'em kill each other. Saves us the trouble."

I wrote an eloquent report on the *999th Strafregiment*, which no doubt ended up in someone's "in" basket or waste basket. Same difference. A substantial number of anti-Nazi POWs were killed by their fellow prisoners in camps ostensibly run by the U.S. Army, both in the States and in Europe, but to the best of my knowledge no official figures have ever been released.

Lt. Raymond Doester, being near-pathologically sane, was totally out of place in this setup, though it would be difficult to conceive of one likely to accommodate him. Dutch-born, schooled in France, he had studied physics at Princeton and was both a scientific whiz and a mechanical genius, reason enough for the army to assign him to military intelligence as a language expert in French and German. French he knew. Not only was he fluent in the language, but he also had a thorough grounding in French literature that eventually helped me make up for some conspicuous gaps in my own education. In German, on the other hand, he was totally lost, but way back some bright boy in Personnel had decided that Dutch was *deutsch*, and *deutsch* was what they spoke in Berlin, so . . .

We became close friends. Aside from an occasional POW interrogation, we were in charge of CS—the Countersubversive Section, also and more aptly known as the Siesta Section, which entailed the collection and tabulation of monthly reports from unit intelligence officers throughout the Theater of Operations concerning potentially subversive elements in their outfits. There never were any such elements, or at least none detected by the fine-meshed network of inept stoolies and their reluctant handlers that were supposed to ferret them out, but the reports were due nonetheless on the first of each month, a pointless peristalsis moving up the line from company to battalion to regiment only to finally end up with me, the enemy alien of a mere year ago now gleefully sitting on top of the shitpile. Impressive, careerwise, whatever it may say about military intelligence. Aside from the couple of hours it took to draw up the monthly "nothing to report" report replete with the usual irrelevant statistics to be sent to Algiers, we were pretty much on our own the rest of the time. I haunted the Tunis bookshops, Raymond haunted the junkyards full of wrecked vehicles and put together a German jeep, prototype of the Volkswagen, for our personal transportation. We liberated a shortwave radio and spent much of the summer reading and writing. I ploughed through whatever French and American literature we could get hold of and, aside from writing daily letters home, worked on a number of short stories lost to the world because I entrusted them to a doe-eyed Red Cross worker who was dying to read them and instead vanished with the only copies I had. She was no loss, and neither, I suspect, were the stories.

Staff conference with our French counterpart, the *Deuxième Bureau*, anxious to alert the U.S. Army, the U.S. government, and the American people to the grave danger represented by the Arab independence movement. Like our own FBI files under the dirty old closet fag who ran The Bureau throughout the war and for decades thereafter, theirs focused heavily on the sexual proclivities of the leading subversives; all smutty minds wallow in similar ruts. And I am sure J. Edgar would have cordially endorsed the sentiment of the introduction to the first dossier I translated: "*L'arabe ment comme il respire*—to the Arab, lying is like breathing." Except that instead of Ayrabs he would have picked on blacks.

The irony of that particular attitude being that there were only two men in the entire unit who did any kind of more or less useful work, and both of them were black. In part this had to do with the nature of their assignment; rather than chasing phantasmagoric spies and subversives, they tracked real corruption, payoffs, black-marketeering and assorted fraud, of which there was more than enough for them to handle. But beyond keeping busy unlike the rest of us, Smitty and The Duke were quite simply the most mature and the most competent members of the unit by far, and accepted as such by everyone, including the colonel, who let his unacknowledged awe slip out in a memorable and much quoted sentence: "If they wasn't niggers, they'd already be generals."

As is, they were sergeants, the only men with the background and training relevant to their job—Smitty a Des Moines P.D. detective with a law degree, The Duke an undercover investigator from Washington, D.C. with a secondary career as a jazz pianist. Far more impressive than their formal credentials, however, were personality traits the more conspicuous for being indefinable and which had gained them universal respect and admiration in a white world biased beyond anything imaginable nowadays in the integrated army. They had each of them seen more of life than all the rest of us put together—but they couldn't have coffee with us in the same Red Cross Service Club.

The eight other enlisted men were a pleasant but nondescript bunch, with the exception of R. Preston Walker, editor of the Grand Junction, Colorado *Daily Sentinel* and son of the paper's founder-owner. The *Sentinel* was the only liberal, openly Democratic daily being published on the western slope of the Rockies, defiantly pro-Roosevelt, and Pres had obviously inherited much of his father's streak of wayward orneriness. Though already past draft age and, moreover, disqualified on medical grounds, he managed to argue his way into the Air Force and after some major disagreements with his superiors ended up in military intelligence. In theory, he was to write up the weekly activity reports, but since in practice there was no activity to report, he wrote articles and editorials for the *Sentinel* instead, played blackjack and smoked two packs a day to keep himself away from liquor. He was, underneath his gruff, tough hombre Western pose, an uncommonly generous and warm-hearted soul who hated cant, preachers and Republicans; Ruth and I visited him after the war and even briefly contemplated settling in Grand Junction. Pres died in his fifties of a heart attack while shooting the rapids on the Snake River—precisely the way he would have wanted to go, except that it could have waited another twenty years. Then again, you can't have everything, not in life and not in death, either.

In February '44 I received notice via the Red Cross that my mother was to undergo surgery but that no emergency home leave could be granted because in the surgeon's judgment the illness was terminal and my presence would not affect the outcome. This did not prevent him from going ahead just the same and operating not once but twice, the second time with fatal results.

Her death, at the age of fifty-two, affected me far more profoundly than I think I was prepared to acknowledge at the time even—and most particularly—to myself. I mourned her, with that mixture of self-pity inseparable from mourning, but the true extent of the loss did not make itself felt until much later. There was more than an ocean separating me from her death, a distance transcending mere space. Ours was a relationship so free of open friction on the surface that at the time I simply failed to perceive its shoals and intricate complexities. She had none of the hysterical egotism, the unmet needs and self-centered vanity that masquerade as mother love, and the intrusive possessiveness so persistently—and unfairly—ascribed to the stereotype of the Jewish mother was totally alien to her entire being. She would undoubtedly have respected my independence even if our special circumstances had not forced the issue long before it ever should have become one, but I suspect that what I saw as an affectionate if somewhat remote relationship evolving out of the intimacy of early childhood must have struck her as a deliberate withdrawal, a willful effort on my part to keep her out of those aspects of my life that really mattered. She was probably right—and hurting. But much too discreet to protest.

None of which changes the fact that, *pace Freud*, it was she who wielded the decisive influence in my formative years; my father's impact on my character development was slight and benign if largely negative in that I resented his easygoing optimism and his readiness for compromise. And while I now tend to believe that Oedipus is more myth than complex, I came to discover after her death that my mother had been infinitely closer and more important to me than I ever realized.

Resistant as the army bureaucracy—like any bureaucracy—was to common sense, by April of 1944 even its nitwits-in-command apparently realized that the whole system of personnel selection, with its for its time sophisticated IBM punchcards, had broken down and that the only way to locate people with special skills was to send interviewers out into the field. The captain from Allied Force Headquarters who one April morning quizzed me about Yugoslavia, the political situation, and my knowledge of the language obviously knew his business and in parting volunteered that I would soon be reassigned to where that knowledge could be put to use.

The meaning was unmistakable, but it left open the question of which guerrilla forces I was going to deal with. Draga Mikhajlovich's Chetniks, still recognized by us as the official Royal Yugoslav Army, had their headquarters in Cairo, while Tito's Partisans were being supplied through their base in Bari, Italy. I had no use for the Chetniks but would have loved to have gone to Cairo, for its own sake and because it was but a few hours by jeep from Palestine. On the other hand there was Italy and the Partisans . . .

I would have had a hard time making the choice, but it was made for me. On a bright morning at the end of April I left Tunis on the first plane ride of my life, and an hour later we buzzed the Bay of Naples, with Mt. Vesuvius in the background.

5. *(Above)* Ernst Pawel
with his mother (1942).

6. With Ruth (1942).

7. With Gigitte (1943).

8. In Africa (1943).

9. In Bari (1944).

10. c. 1951.

11. In Jerusalem in 1987.

NINETEEN

I t was my great good fortune to land in Naples with orders to report to an outfit no one had ever heard of. As a result the Army Transportation Center, not knowing what to do with me and much too busy to care, arranged for meals and temporary housing and told me to get lost for the time being. I was to drift in bureaucratic limbo until they caught up with me, a homeless transient with two barracks bags containing all my earthly possessions, including my own personnel file, without which I would never even be missed till long after the war was over. As it turned out, it took the Army an entire week to get me back on track, and I made the most of it.

Never, before or since, have I experienced so heady a sense of total freedom.

Partly no doubt a matter of being on my own, for the first time in years, with a room in a sleazy hotel by the railroad station, a pass to an Air Force mess in case I got tired of black-market restaurants, and no duties or responsibilities whatsoever other than putting in an appearance at the Transportation office every other day. Fuzzy, furry U.S. Army, mother of the Welfare State.

Much more important, though, was Napoli, the capital of anarchy with its intoxicating blend of vitality and chaos, just emerging from the war as from a nightmare. The slum districts had sustained heavy damage and casualties in Allied bombings, and the retreating Germans, after executing hundreds of hostages, blew up a number of public buildings and left time bombs in others; days after their departure a delayed explosion wrecked the main post office and killed dozens of civilians. But the heart of the city, with its eclectic mix of baroque grandeur and fascist megalomania, was by then caught up in an explosion of a different kind, an ecstatic round-the-clock street party celebrating life, liberty and the pursuit of whatever you could lay your hands on, while in the battered tenements and hovels of the suburbs people were content merely to have survived, a trick they had performed time and again over the past few thousand years and which did not strike them as a cause for special celebration. To them the Allies were just another round of the recurrent plague, another horde of barbarians even if their wealth and technological sophistication posed some new challenges. But having honed their skills through the ages, the local survivalists soon learned to dismantle and steal entire trucks without so much as waking the driver.

Walking the streets from morning to night, climbing Mount Vesuvius, hitching rides to Pompeii, Amalfi and Positano, swimming in the Gulf of Naples, I briefly succumbed to the tourist vision of Italy, a compound of enthusiasm and innocence I was never quite able to recapture in later years, and not only because one can no longer imagine the Amalfi drive without a traffic jam. The essence of Italy has little to do with the landscape; Switzerland can boast of more majestic views. But Switzerland is full of Swiss.

Whereas Italy has the Italians. Who, when all is said that can be said about the Mafia and Mussolini, about Camorra and corruption, are probably the most civilized people in Europe. Certainly the most human.

A week later, having located me on the map, a surly dispatcher shipped me off to Sorrento for a briefing at G-2 Headquarters. From there I and my barracks bags, duly briefed, bounced across the peninsula in a courier truck and arrived in Bari seven hours later with scrambled innards and mixed emotions. The driver dumped me on the sidewalk in front of the fascist-monumentalist post office in the center of town, and the first people I saw were two Yugoslav Partisans, one a giant toting a Sten gun, the other limping along on crutches.

I had come full circle.

My mission was to recruit and supervise a civilian staff which, jointly with members of the Yugoslav People's Army of Liberation, as the Partisans were formally known, was to screen all messages—letters, cards and other missives, down to the last desperate scraps of paper—being smuggled by the bagful every week out of the German-occupied Balkans for information of potential military significance. The project, conceived in the rarified atmosphere of high-level obscurantism, testified to a fatuous ignorance of the facts on the ground; whoever cooked it up didn't have a clue as to what the Partisans were all about. To Tito and his hard-core Communist leadership, we represented the enemy, despite a temporary tactical alliance born of the need for logistic support. And although forced to agree to the joint censorship operation—it was Allied planes, after all, that brought out most of the mail—they were convinced that we were out fishing for political rather than military intelligence, and that it was their job to foil our sinister plot to the best of their ability. When it came to ignorance, parochialism and sheer stupidity, both sides seemed to me pretty well matched, but the Partisans, in addition, brought to this mission a degree of paranoia that mocked any pretense at cooperation.

All of which seemed self-evident from the start. But what turned our first formal meeting into a disaster and almost scuttled the whole project was not Partisan pigheadedness so much as the presence of my new superior officer. You didn't have to be paranoid to be thrown by Navy Lieutenant Sheridan "Call me Sherry" H. Ward.

I have no idea how Naval Intelligence got involved in the Balkan censorship project; for all I know, it was their idea to begin with. In any case, Sherry Ward was in many ways their rather typical representative: an upper-class WASP and closet homosexual about ten years my senior, with a Princeton degree and a voluble dedication to the teachings of the late but immortal Mary Baker Eddy; his religious fervor provided an impregnable crust of intellectual smugness and moral superiority. In civilian life Sherry had been a travel agent specializing in Yugoslavia, a country which for some mysterious reason held an abiding fascination for him; not only had his M.A. thesis dabbled in Yugoslav history, but he had also memorized a few phrases in Serbo-Croatian, a feat that apparently impressed Naval Intelligence to the point of singling him out for this assignment.

Our initial meeting with the Partisans took place the day after my arrival. Five of their officers, headed by a lieutenant colonel, came stomping into our office, life-sized wooden soldiers uniformly grim-faced and dour, clearly under orders to betray no human emotions in the face of the cunning capitalists. They introduced themselves, and it came as something of a shock to realize that one of them, a skeletal apparition with a shaved head and the fiercest scowl by far, seemed to be a

woman. As it turned out, Comrade Dragitsa was actually a Sarajevo teenager recovering from typhoid fever and a winter of
war in the Bosnian mountains, and we later became good
friends, but at the outset her principled hostility made cooperation rather difficult.

We assembled in the plush conference room of the post
office, and I was about to start outlining the agenda when the
colonel took a bulky album from his briefcase and with a loud
thud dropped it on the table. "The Black Book of German
Atrocities," he announced, opening the album and shoving it
under Sherry Ward's nose. "Before we discuss technicalities I
want you to take a look at this, so you know our common
enemy. All authentic documents. Most of the photographs
were taken by the very monsters who perpetrated these bes-
tialities."

Sherry resolutely shook his head. "I am not allowed to look
at these," he declared.

The colonel's jaw dropped.

"It's against my religion," Sherry amplified, which added
nothing to anyone's understanding.

"Religion?" asked the colonel, incredulous.

"I am a Christian Scientist," Sherry said, with a touch of defiance which, to give him the benefit of the doubt, may have
masked a fleeting sense of embarrassment on his part but didn't
make my job any easier. A mere literal translation of the term
would have struck these people as utterly meaningless; they
knew many scientists who considered themselves Christians
without therefore refusing to face bloody facts. Thus, although I
had only a very sketchy notion of Mary Baker Eddy's teachings
and no inclination whatsoever to defend them, I found myself
in the uncomfortable position of having to explain her basic
ideas to the best of my ability, a matter of playing saint's advo-
cate in a court of Marxist skeptics. They listened gravely, but

neither their attempt to comprehend the incomprehensible nor my struggle to explain the inexplicable got any of us very far.

"Ask him, the colonel finally interrupted, gesturing in Sherry's direction, "if he knows that war is about killing people. Because if they didn't die, as he says, then what the hell are we doing here?"

Sherry, with all the passion of a Princetonian cheerleader, was about to launch into a defense of the Mother Church, but I was in no mood to referee a fight of competing theologies bound to end in a walkout by the prickly Partisians and suggested instead that we get down to business. The response from the comrade colonel was a weirdly complicit glance which in effect sealed an entente of sorts between us; he had evidently let himself admit the possibility of Sherry being just what he appeared to be—a harmless fool.

"All right, then, let's get started."

The speed with which we assembled a staff and the relative ease with which we operated for nearly ten months as a joint unit with little serious friction owed far more, I think, to the Partisans' assessment of Sherry Ward than to my feeble attempts at dispelling their paranoia; paranoid or not, they were bright enough to realize that a clown like Sherry could be a lot more useful to them than the politically sophisticated cynics of the various British intelligence services they had to deal with. The other reason for our amiable relations was the utter futility and the complete failure of communications on which this entire project was based. On the Allied side, the professed intent was to glean information of potentially strategic significance. The Partisans, on the other hand, read the mail—meticulously, be it said—with only one purpose in mind: to find evidence of pro- or anti-Tito sentiment. The passages praising Tito formed the substance of their daily and weekly communiqués;

the anti-Tito missives were presumably passed on to their own embryonic organs of internal security. Our own civilian censors—Yugoslav refugees who, under the agreement, had to be approved by the Partisans—shared a similar monomaniacal focus on politics, and time and again would triumphantly present me with some rambling diatribe against the Germans while overlooking the potentially useful factual information contained in the same letter. But as long as the Partisans felt that the joint operations gave them a means to impress us with their domestic support, they were happy to cooperate. What, if anything, we got out of them I don't know.

Both Sherry and I had to submit regular monthly reports to headquarters. Sherry, in a self-conscious effort to stress his distinctive status as an outsider—no illiterate army prole he—entitled his reports "Vignettes of Life in Bari." (He was right on target. At a staff meeting in Rome some months later, the colonel in charge wanted to know if vignettes were something you ate in the Navy. "Goddamn things give me indigestion.") My own reports were always drafted in scrupulously basic militarese, but I soon found that the information collected by reading other people's mail was meager indeed compared to what one could pick up every day, and especially every night, in various places around town. And as I myself became part of the scene, I tried to do it justice in ever longer memos to headquarters. I don't know to what extent I succeeded, nor whether anyone ever even read them. At the time I thought it mattered.

TWENTY

Bari, though an ancient crusader port with a richly checkered past—Illyrian, Greek, Roman, Norman, Byzantine and fascist among many others—is nonetheless largely bereft of charm, except perhaps for its famous basilica housing what are purported to be the mortal remains of St. Nicholas, alias Santa Claus, the fourth-century bishop of Myra in what is now Turkey. In 1087 a gang of Barese sailors stole the by then sainted bones and took them home with them, an exploit the town still celebrates every May with a three-day feast that draws pilgrims from all over the country.

At one point during World War II, however, Bari fleetingly acquired a distinctly cosmopolitan allure as its population nearly doubled and it hosted, or was forced to host, an improbable assortment of military units, acronymic agencies, spy outfits, freelance operators, secret and not-so-secret agents, black marketeers, refugees and fugitives from dozens of nations. Aside from British and American troops, the place was teeming with soldiers and civilians from practically every nation involved in the war—Yugoslavs, Greeks, Albanians, New Zealanders, Poles, Czechs, Australians as well as members of the Jewish Brigade recruited in Palestine—who turned the broad central *corso* into a colorful promenade during the day and a freak show at night when, for want of Germans, they started fighting each other. But it was an altogether different army, an army of women, poor and young women above all, many of them barely into their teens, who charged the atmosphere with vibrancy and predatory tension and made the whole town come alive. They flocked to Bari from all over what was—and still is— Italy's notoriously poorest province, driven by hunger, despair or rebellion, lured by dreams and delusions. Although quite a few did find temporary employment in military installations, many others drifted into prostitution, but a surprising number settled into stable, monogamous relationships, especially with British and American officers and enlisted men. A few of these liaisons led to marriage, the rest ended when orders came to move on, with regrets and a few babies as lasting reminders of what passes for love in time of war. To me the most moving aspect of these on their face often crudely mercenary arrangements was the emotional generosity of the women; by and large, what they gave of themselves seemed infinitely more precious than what they received in return. Yet not all of it was wasted; quite a few boys from Leeds or Liverpool or Pittsburgh were, I think, permanently changed for the better by a touch of grace and humanity they never expected and seldom deserved.

I shared a by Barese standards fairly modern eight-room apartment near the center of town with two British members of the Allied Control Commission and three Italian-American GIs, natives of Bari familiar with the local Greco-Albanian dialect who, among other, more lucrative private occupations, also worked for the Psychological Warfare Section. Thanks to their contacts we were able to hire a cook and supplement the army-supplied rations with an abundance of local fare. As the latest arrival I was given the huge front parlor stuffed with period furniture, including a silk-covered semicircular love seat on which it would seem difficult to make love but on which I somehow managed to sleep for months without getting permanently bent out of shape. This, however, was about the worst hardship I had to endure; on the whole, with a car, a chauffeur, a plush office and far more money than I had any reason to spend, I lived better in Bari than I ever had in my life, as far as outward circumstances were concerned.

My social adjustment, on the other hand, turned out to be more complicated than in my naiveté I had anticipated; it took time for me to realize that in this climate of rampant paranoia everyone was guilty until proven innocent. Paranoids do have enemies, and where they don't, they usually manage to create them, so that it would have been unfair to blame the Partisans for regarding anyone with as murky a background as mine with considerable suspicion. They were anxious to know who I *really* was, and by that they meant my politics; the Partisan view of the human psyche was flat-earth red-and-white, dividing humanity into progressives versus reactionaries and into heroes versus cowards. In my case, they were somewhat handicapped in their customary methods of investigation, a cute habit they had of simply kidnapping people whose background they deemed suspicious. They therefore went for hospitality and good feelings instead and turned an elaborate luncheon at Partisan Headquarters into a devious kind of cross-examination, feigning a lively curiosity about my Belgrade years. Since I assumed that they already knew all there was to know about that distant past from people who remembered me, I made it a point to be as candid as possible about it. But when they began to question me about my life in the States, I had to tread carefully, a tightrope walker without a safety net. I could not afford to appear as either anti-Stalinist or fellow-traveling; both perceptions would have made my job impossible. Above all, no mention of the one who, in their cosmology, had become Lucifer incarnate, conspiring even from beyond the grave against the fatherland of socialism. Any contamination by Trotsky's ideas called for prophylactic liquidation, and any favorable or even neutral reference to him would have been tantamount to inviting a fatal accident.

The image I strove to project in the end, while fudging some of the more salient features, was not too far removed from the truth. At any rate, it seemed to satisfy the Partisans, even though from time to time Comrade Marko, the resident commissar of our unit, saw fit to retest my allegiance, usually by asking me to check on the whereabouts of some "well-known war criminal now working for Western intelligence." I would simply pass the request on up the line and so inform Comrade Marko. He wasn't terribly swift, but he eventually got the message and gave up on me, though he never stopped to wonder out loud how a progressive person, himself a victim of fascism, no less, could refuse to serve the cause.

As for Western intelligence, they did in due course recruit an amazing collection of war criminals and other human trash, but in Bari at the time the only organizations to whom the word intelligence could be applied without provoking helpless mirth were a few small and exceedingly discreet British outfits. Britain, in contrast to the United States—where, according to Navy Secretary Stimson speaking in the 1920s, "gentlemen don't read other people's mail"—had a long tradition of espionage and took care to choose and train its practitioners well ahead of time. Many of the academics commissioned at the outbreak of the war and attached to the several British missions had studied in prewar Yugoslavia, no doubt on special stipends, and were reasonably familiar with the country, the people and the language. Though left out of the censorship project, they considered "the Jugs" their own particular bailiwick, but far from giving vent to their resentment, they instead welcomed us with the sort of donnish snobbery that the uninitiated easily mistake for kindness. Sherry was quickly disposed of; it took them mere minutes to grasp the full scope of his ignorance; with me, on the other hand, they were wary—every bit as suspicious as the Partisans, but much more intelligent about it. They had good reason too. With few exceptions, they were heavily left-leaning and passionately pro-Partisan, and the last thing in the world they needed was some meddlesome Yank creating problems for them.

The general drift of things was instantly apparent, and so were some very outspoken Stalinists among both officers and enlisted men. One of them, a former editor of the *London Daily Worker* teaching sabotage techniques along the Dalmatian coast, became a close friend and roomed with me whenever he came back to the base in Bari. It may well be that the mission's reports contributed their share to certain top-level policy decisions, but to credit the likes of a Captain Klugman with having been instrumental in shifting Allied support from Drazha Mihajlovich's Chetniks to Tito's Partisans testifies to the kind of pervasive ignorance and ideological blindness that have characterized most retrospective debates on the subject. From the perspective of 1944, at any rate, it seemed obvious that the Partisans, whether or not we chose to support them, were the only effective force fighting the Germans in the Balkans. They also happened to be the only one struggling to overcome the murderous tribalism that even then had turned the country into a slaughterhouse. Fashionable though it now may be to blame Tito for the breakup of Yugoslavia and for the triumph of barbarism in its wake, the fact is that the same gangs of cutthroats, rapists, thieves, perverts, arsonists and assassins who currently pass themselves off as patriot killers in whatever holy cause were already perpetrating mass murder during the Second World War. That the Communists brutally suppressed them is true. Whether they had a choice is at least open to question. But to ascribe the bestiality of the current crop of Chetniks, Ustashis and assorted gangsters to Communist repression demonstrates a simple-minded ideological bias that avoids coming to grips with far more basic and infinitely more disturbing questions.

I don't know when exactly my probationary period came to an end. The Brits loosened up very quickly, although—paranoia being highly contagious—I was never quite sure if they befriended me on orders or out of genuine sympathy. The Partisans took a little longer, but after a couple of weeks the ice around me began to break up and I suddenly found myself back among the teenage companions of my Belgrade years. And although the ghosts far outnumbered the living, some of them were still triumphantly alive.

Despite the cosmopolitan mix of Bari's transient population, there was little opportunity for contact among the different groups. The service clubs were strictly segregated by rank as well as nationality, housing shortages and black-market rivalries strained relations between the Bari natives and civilian refugees, and the amenities for a more or less normal existence—food, fuel and cafés—were in very short supply. Under the circumstances, the emergence of the Jewish Club as the focal point of social life had about it a certain inevitability, the only place in town where everyone was welcome, regardless of status, nationality, rank, religion, prior or present convictions.

The club occupied a four-story building in the center of town and was ostensibly run by the Jewish community, which in fact operated a soup kitchen for refugees in the basement as well as the coffee bar on the main floor, where crowds assembled every night in a cozy haze of cigarette smoke and carried on multilingual conversations that in all innocence sometimes led nowhere.

But not everyone came there to socialize, as it turned out. The exuberant party atmosphere on the two lower floors was meant to camouflage activities on the two upper ones, which served as a combination safe house and nerve center for rescue operations involving Jewish agents and emissaries from Palestine. Israeli intelligence, now by sheer force of necessity one of the most efficient in the world, was in its embryonic beginnings in 1944, run by an assortment of rank amateurs and indiscreet bumblers bloated with self-importance who violated the most elementary rules of secrecy. Anyone who joined the crowd on the lower floors had no trouble finding out what was going on up above. Moreover, if the anyone happened to be female and willing to get laid, all she had to do was walk upstairs and knock on the door to be admitted; those not-so-secret agents made it a point to advertise their indiscriminate horniness, and judging from the steady traffic up and down those stairs they had a fair number of presumably satisfied customers. But it was in those same rooms that most Jewish volunteers, among them Hannah Senesh and Enzo Sereni, spent their tense last days waiting for the signal to be infiltrated or dropped behind enemy lines.

Once there, they were quickly caught and put to death as spies.

Where we failed to see the enemy in front of our nose, the Partisans saw enemies everywhere. The seasoned veterans of the Communist underground who ran the movement were conditioned to suspect everybody, and some old habits, like some old party hacks, never die. In the long run, their paranoia helped to wreck their country; in the short run, it had a certain survival value, and we would have done well to curb our own tendency to smugness and be a little more security-minded. We more than made up for it later on, in the years of the cold war.

I don't know exactly when and on what basis I was eventually cleared by the Partisan KGB and pronounced fit for human contact, but a few weeks after my arrival four of my old Belgrade comrades from the Zionist youth movement suddenly showed up at the Jewish Club looking for me. It was a dramatic moment, rendered the more intense for being deliberately underplayed by all of us to begin with; they wore the Partisan uniform, I was an American GI, and somehow we all felt the need to act our part. But it did not take long for the synthetic ice to melt; by midnight we were just ourselves again, a handful of survivors.

It turned out that they were all in Bari on temporary assignment. Yehuda, the bespectacled intellectual with a penchant for Talmudic sophistry, was taking a course in automotive maintenance—badly needed in an army of peasants who treated what vehicles we provided with withering contempt and could not be persuaded to ever check the oil. Atsa, a once irrepressible clown who had long since run out of jokes, was being trained in radio communications, and the other two were doing clerical work at base headquarters while recovering from wounds, disease, lice and hunger.

They filled me in at last about events in Belgrade, starting with the saturation bombing by the *Luftwaffe* on Easter Sunday of 1941 that destroyed half the city and killed some twenty thousand people. A week later the victorious Nazi army set up a fascist puppet regime under the leadership of one General Nedich and began rounding up Belgrade's Jews who, along with Communists and anti-Nazi patriots, were interned on the old Zemun fairgrounds across the river. A few survived long enough to be shipped later to the industrialized death camps to the east, but by and large the killing in Zemun as well as in Jasenovac, its Croatian counterpart, was done by hand, with an individualized bestiality in sharp contrast to the impersonal methods of mass murder perpetrated by the Nazis and foreshadowing the medieval atrocities of our own day. Among the early victims was Geza Kon, whose custom-built Mercedes became the German *Stadtkommandant*'s personal conveyance. A number of younger Jews managed to escape into the underground, but even among them the losses were heavy; the rest, the vast majority, perished in short order.

As we talked, we were all acutely aware that, like most survivors, we had been spared mainly by luck and that none of our conscious decisions had had much to do with it. And yet guilt defies reason; they had lost parents, siblings and lovers, and could never quite stop blaming themselves even while they knew better. "If I hadn't left them and headed for the woods . . ."

"You wouldn't be here, either."

"Maybe I oughtn't to be."

During the early days of the German occupation, the Yugoslav *Hashomer Hatzair* formally joined the underground resistance movement being organized under the leadership of the Communist Party, which promised that any survivors still wishing to emigrate after the war would be permitted to do so. On the whole, they kept their word, and contact between Israeli and Yugoslav Jews remained close even after the 1967 suspension of diplomatic relations between the two countries. In June '41, on orders from a Kremlin desperate to stem the German advance on Moscow, the Partisans launched their armed resistance ahead of schedule. Inadequate preparations, a shortage of arms and a lack of combat experience resulted in devastating losses, and most of our Belgrade comrades were killed in the early battles around the capital.

We ended up in my room that night, all five of us, talking till dawn. Our way of burying the dead.

The Bari spring of 1944 was short-lived but exhilarating while it lasted, smiles and handshakes all around, cooperation and promises of a common great, glorious and peaceful future. Rome liberated, the Allies landing in Normandy, Tito meets Churchill and agrees to a coalition government in Yugoslavia as well as to parliamentary elections and a plebiscite on the monarchy. After the war, that is; meanwhile the little boy who ten years earlier had followed the coffin of his murdered father through Belgrade's streets and who had spent the war in the safety of the English countryside could dream of coming back home to the acclamation of his grateful subjects and reclaim his throne. King Peter II of Yugoslavia. Tito sealed the agreement with a limp handshake and a sardonic smile; he knew full well who the king of postwar Yugoslavia was going to be. What is more, he already looked the part.

In Bari that spring, *mirabile dictu*, it was possible for me to be friends with members of the PLA—the People's Liberation Army—without exposing them to any major sanctions. The commissars, though vigilant as always, were temporarily muzzled, and my old *Hashomer Hatzair* buddies from Belgrade didn't much care, anyway. They retained a certain critical distance from the Communist leadership even while remaining fiercely loyal to the cause. Comrade Dragitsa, on the other hand, and her crew of censors culled from the innermost circle of the faithful never voiced any but the most worshipful sentiments about Comrade Tito and his apostles. Yet with her hair grown back and her face filling out, Dragitsa within a matter of weeks underwent a miraculous transformation from androgy-

nous skeleton to a pert young woman with a surprisingly mis-
chievous sparkle in her eyes that somehow contradicted the
relentless platitudes she felt obliged to spout whenever the conversation veered toward politics and the war. She, too, began to
relax that spring, and our hitherto very official relations gradually became human to the point where she would actually have
tea alone with me in my office. I learned that she had been in
her last year of high school in Karlovac, a small town in Croatia,
when the war broke out. The Ustashe killed her father, a Serb,
as well as her older brother, even though the mother was a
Croat. Dragitsa "took to the woods," as they say, along with half
her class, eight boys and five girls, of whom she now, three
years into the war, was the only survivor. Months later—we had
become real friends by then—I once asked her what she was
going to do after the war. "Be an old woman and tend to the
graves," she said. "There will be so few old women and so many
graves."

Cassandra silencing the commissar. And looking fifty years
into the future.

The godless Communist Partisan army enforced chastity with
a rigor that should have impressed the current Pope as well as
certain radical feminists: capital punishment for sexual intercourse within the unit. The measure may seem draconian in retrospect and certainly had a distinct finality about it, but in the
context of guerrilla warfare few other punishments are feasible,
and no army in the field had ever faced a comparable challenge.
Partly for ideological reasons, echoes of the *Urkommunismus*
of pre-Stalin days with its notions of sexual equality, but more
specifically for purely practical ones—there was no front line,
then as now, hence no safe rear echelon—men and women
fought, bled, starved and died together in mixed units that were
forever on the move, hunters and hunted at once, in the unfor-

giving seasons of a land without mercy. Under the circumstances, sexual liaisons would have undermined morale, and
pregnancies made for potential disaster. Married couples were
separated and assigned to different units.

One man's crime is another man's privilege; it always depends
on who it is that draws the distinction. Comrade Tito was, of
course, above suspicion; he slept with Tigar, the German shepherd that saved his life during the Drvar offensive, while Herta,
his second wife (he divorced three times), remained in hiding
throughout the war, and the multilingual, beautiful Olga
Ninchich served as his personal secretary. How scrupulously
lesser leaders or ordinary fighters, having no dogs to sleep
with, observed the rule of abstinence I have no way of knowing. The Partisans kept no record of formal or informal execu-
tions, and demoralizing rumors were dealt with every bit as
sternly as unauthorized screwing, but I suspect that in the field
at least cold, hunger and fear greatly helped keep the problem
to manageable proportions.

In Bari, however, the edict was discreetly and selectively
ignored. My most intimate friend among the local Partisan staff
came to be Colonel Jacob A., the chief medical officer of the
base, who lived with his wife in a requisitioned private apartment they shared with the deaf old lady who owned it. Jacob, a
young Sephardic Jew practicing medicine in his native Zagreb,
took to the woods immediately after the outbreak of the war
and joined the Partisans together with his wife. For some two
years they served in separate units until Zora came down with a
bad case of typhoid fever. Against all expectations she pulled
through but developed a series of complications for which she
had to be evacuated to the Partisan base hospital; her husband's
Bari assignment was a rare gesture of compassion from up high.

The two of them became my adoptive family in Bari, and
almost every night on my way home I would stop off at their

place to listen to the 11 P.M. BBC news and to Jacob's commentary on the day's happenings in his hospital and the world on the other shore of the Adriatic. He was a short and compact man, dark-skinned, with a shock of black hair and eyes that seemed to glow in the dark, but what had once been an impish sense of humor had turned bitter and acquired a cutting edge that he wielded like a scalpel. He, too, was circumspect with me in the beginning, but once we grew close he did not hesitate to vent his feelings, which by then had reached a near-critical mass. There was no question about his unconditional loyalty to the Partisan movement; as a Jew and a free-wheeling democratic leftist he regarded the war as a holy crusade, but he was the first to point out to me many of the incipient problems—the personality cult, the thought police, the totalitarian mindcast of the leadership and its intellectual inflexibility—that were to assume catastrophic proportions after the war.

I was probably at that time the only one with whom he felt free to talk, and it took me a while to realize that the warm welcome I received every night reflected not only his and his wife's fondness for me but also the sense of relief at not having to spend the evening alone with each other.

It was Zora who eventually made me her uneasy confidant and told me a great deal more about their marriage than I wanted to know. But once she got going, there was no stopping her, and though I felt rather ill-equipped for the task of marital counseling, it soon became clear that her litany of complaints had little to do with either her husband or the marriage but was simply a desperate lashing out against fate on the part of a young woman physically ill and emotionally brutalized by two years of war in which she had often been in blood up to her elbows. Jacob did what he could for her as a physician and as a husband. He loved her, but neither love nor vitamin injections proved quite enough to heal the heart and soul of a pampered rich little girl who at twenty-four took to the woods with a fur jacket and her one pair of low-heeled shoes, spent the next two years tending to the dead and dying in the mountains of Bosnia and ended up near death herself. Zora did recover sufficiently to give birth to a daughter after the war, but she herself died a few years later, still in her thirties.

TWENTY-ONE

The Partisans' base hospital in Grumo, some twenty miles south of Bari, essentially focused on convalescence and rehabilitation, the speedy evacuation of acute cases in the field being virtually impossible until very late in the war. Jacob had every right to be proud of that hospital, in whose concept he had been the guiding spirit; in certain aspects of care it was decidedly ahead of its time, especially if one takes into account what now, a mere half century later, strikes us as the primitive state of medicine in those prehistoric days. Having no miracle pills to peddle—neither antibiotics nor antidepressants were as yet available—physicians were forced to come up with more imaginative ways of coping with the physical and emotional aftermath of trauma. At Grumo all patients, chiefly amputees and typhus survivors, were given chores that kept them out of bed and busy most of the day, while the evenings were devoted to lectures and movies. The therapeutic goal was to prevent invalidism, self-pity and depression by maintaining a high level

of collective enthusiasm. Fair enough. But as in so many other
Partisan initiatives, lofty ideals, base instincts and mindless
bureaucracy combined in unpredictable ways, and though I
spent quite a bit of time in Grumo—Jacob bludgeoned me into
giving some lectures on American politics and trade union-
ism—I have no idea to what extent these measures actually succeeded. True, there never was heard a discouraging word, but
the pervasive system of thought control with its sanctions and
its network of at that stage still predominantly voluntary and
ideologically motivated informers made it impossible to tell
how these men and women really felt.

Privately, several of my friends expressed guarded criticism
and reservations—"My army is bigger than yours. Your Ike is
just a general, our Tito is a marshal. And even his goddamn dog
has been promoted to a national hero"—but most of it
amounted to no more than the sort of griping that any army
takes for granted. The fact that the PLA so vigorously suppressed it was, or should have been, a fairly clear indication of
what the future held in store.

Still, even those whose brains remained refreshingly unwashed
and who kept their distance from the relatively crude propaganda remained unshaken in their support of Tito as the only
hope for *any* kind of future, given the alternatives. Yet one of
his decisions confronted especially the Jews among them with
an agonizing dilemma. In the late summer of '44, i.e., at a time
when the ultimate outcome of the war was no longer in serious
doubt, the Partisan supreme command offered a limited-time
amnesty to any Ustasha or Chetnik who switched sides and
joined the Partisan army; aside from not being asked any questions about the past, the deserter would also retain his rank.
Politically a shrewd move toward ending the civil war-within-a-
war, but one with devastating personal consequences for people who suddenly found themselves outranked and even com-

manded by the very men responsible for the murder of their families. Rumor—impossible to verify, given the Partisan penchant for secrecy—had it that several Croatian-Jewish fighters killed themselves rather than serve under these late-hour converts.

When a German paratroop attack on Drvar early in the year very nearly captured Tito and his entire staff, it was decided to move the Partisan supreme command to the island of Vis, off the coast but still nominally part of Yugoslavia. The air and sea defenses of the island were turned over to the British, who made the most of their mandate, controlling access with a display of harrumping old Empah-building *hauteur*, but guided by policies as confused and confusing as the people who formulated them. At any rate, when the Partisans suggested a visit to the island, I had to get British permission and was turned down flat, no reason given. At the time I wondered if it was the Stalinists or the anti-Titoists who objected, but in all likelihood the decision was simply routine, based on the undeniable fact that I had absolutely no business there and that they did not like people with a suspicious fluency in Serbo-Croatian to go snooping around.

On the American side, our involvement in the Yugoslav situation was at first largely limited to the rescue of air crews whose planes, after bombing raids on targets such as the Ploesti oil fields, couldn't make it back to the Eighth Air Force base at Foggia; Chetniks as well as Partisans had saved hundreds of our men, spurred by the hope of thus earning American support and supplies. But gradually, with the Special Balkan Services being absorbed into the recently organized OSS, there was growing interest in the rapidly evolving internal politics of the country, and some of my reports had apparently caught the attention of the people assigned to dealing with this particularly sticky wicket. In August I was summoned to Rome.

Roma, città aperta—an open city in every sense of the word, and the vision of it in all its supreme if shabby grandeur, still half paralyzed in the wake of its latest liberation, its streets devoid of vehicular traffic but throbbing with life, remains to haunt me in its stark contrast to the metropolis of today, where antiquity and the Middle Ages seem buried under ever more conspicuous encrustations of the present. It was midsummer, and the air heavy with the sweet scent of hope, even in the slums. *Il Duce* was gone, so were the Teutonic barbarians, and the new ones, if nothing else, were generous with their money, cigarettes and chewing gum as they invaded the city. From the flesh market of the Piazza di Spagna all the way up to the Trinità dei Monti the Spanish steps were packed like bleachers with soldiers, racketeers and whores. Bemused, off to one side on the first landing, the ghost of Keats, a still defiant presence in the gloomy room in which he died at the age of twenty-six. *"Poveretto,"* says the curator with much feeling, holding out his hand as I leave, the only visitor all week. I stayed at a picturesquely run-down hotel off the Piazza Navona and explored the city with the frenzied energy of delayed adolescence, layer by layer, from the Roman Forum and the Palatine Hill to the somber menace of St. Peter's. It was Gibbon, whom I didn't read till much later—there is much to be said for a lopsided education that puts first things last—who conveys better than anyone the shock of the encounter with pre-Christian Rome and its abiding resonance through the ages. As a Jew, I have even more reason than Gibbon to take a dim view of Christianity's ascendance over the cosmopolitan civilization of the republic and the early empire, but in a revenge of sorts the once murderous militancy of the Church has been blunted and the Vatican transformed over time into a mere maze of greed, intrigue and hypocrisy.

The official part of the trip was decidedly less exhilarating, a series of meetings and briefings leaving me with the distinct impression that the honeymoon with Tito was about to end and that, as the Allies advanced into northern Italy and the Partisans on the other side of the Adriatic raced them for Trieste, a clash over the future of the city claimed by both Italy and Yugoslavia seemed inevitable. A first glimpse of the postwar world.

At the end of my week in Rome I was told that in view of my good rapport with the Partisans and my language qualifications—by now I also knew Italian reasonably well—I had been picked for a challenging job in Trieste once the city was liberated. The fact that a significant promotion would go with it did not make the prospect seem any less dismal, but I accepted the congratulations with what I hoped was good grace and went back to Bari, the only comforting thought being that we were still very much stuck in Florence, on the southern bank of the Arno.

There were details of life with the Partisans that I did not include in my reports to headquarters.

Such as the sexual problems of the PLA. In the field, as I said, abstinence was the rule, enforced like all rules with relentless rigor. But neither the headquarters staff in Bari nor the hospital personnel in Grumo seemed to feel bound by the chastity pledge, which in any case was dictated by pragmatic needs rather than ideology; when in Italy, do as the Italians do. Unlike their hosts, however, the Yugoslavs were definitely anxious to avoid making *bambini*, but because of an acute shortage of condoms—the only birth control method readily available— they found themselves, according to Jacob, forced to indulge in all sorts of unnatural practices. And although the Allies apparently had ample supplies on hand, neither Jacob nor his colleagues could persuade their top-level liaison people to ask for some Allied lend-lease. Whether they thought it ideologically compromising or were simply embarrassed to bring up the subject is unclear. In any case, it was the only time I ever saw Jacob lose his composure and let fly with a string of invective that covered the entire Partisan high command and would undoubtedly have sufficed to have him shot. "They don't believe in letting people be human," he said, after he calmed down somewhat. "They want goddamn heroes. Supermen. Robots."

He himself very much believed in letting people be human, and between the two of us we worked out a small-scale lend-lease arrangement of our own. There was an Allied Pro-Station on the Via Cairoli, which I passed at least twice a day on my way to and from the office. It was open around the clock and staffed by British noncoms, the idea being for any Allied soldier to be able to walk in and ask for a condom if he contemplated fornication or, if he had already had unprotected intercourse, to get the gonococci and assorted other bugs flushed out of his system before they traveled further upstream. The transaction was deliberately kept anonymous and required no personal contact beyond giving one's serial number.

For weeks on end I stopped in there twice a day, entered my serial number on the register and in return received a condom which I passed on to Jacob. Usually the same two sergeants were on duty every day. Just what they thought of me I can't imagine, but they never uttered a word, never so much as cracked a smile. Professional conduct of the highest order, and a major if unwitting contribution to the morale of a gallant ally.

A contingent of the Palestinian Brigade, including a company of ATS (Army Transport Service) girls, showed up regularly at the Jewish Club. The Palestinian-born among them were predominantly kibbutz members, but somehow the one who became my closest friend also happened to be the one with whom I had the least in common, a fourth-generation Jerusalemite whose English was not much better than my Hebrew but who managed quite eloquently to convey her contempt for Zionism and the Zionists. Her forthright manner and offbeat sense of humor made it easy to bridge the language gap. She explained that she had enlisted mainly as a way of breaking out of the dark world of the ultra-Orthodox in which she had been reared, but the secular pioneers who were transforming the land struck her as equally primitive and brutal. Sonya drove a lorry for a British base hospital in Trani and escaped to Bari whenever she had a chance, and sometimes even when she didn't; the girls in her unit, most of them refugees from Germany and Central Europe who had reached Palestine as teenagers in the thirties and were ardently and volubly Zionist, tended to make things difficult for her. Or rather, she made things difficult for herself, in ways that at the time I was no more equipped to understand than were her comrades, strangers to the medieval mind-set of Jewish ultra-Orthodoxy and the ways in which it permanently scars a woman, most particularly if she has the courage to rebel.

Although the Brigade was part of the British Army, it had a not so hidden agenda of its own. Whatever the motives, mundane or idealistic, that inspired the individual volunteers, the intent of the Zionist leadership was to have them be emissaries to the surviving Jews of Europe and eventually to help rescue the remnants. How much was known by 1944 about the fate of the Jews in Nazi-occupied Europe will forever remain controversial—far more, I would guess, than those in responsible positions of power were subsequently willing to admit. Two points, however, need to be made, neither of which in any way excuses their inaction:

The brutality and scope of the Nazi atrocities simply defied the imagination. As early as the summer of '43 a top-secret intel-

ligence report citing Polish underground sources told of Jews
being gassed by the truckload in specially equipped vans, yet
even I, who had every reason to credit the Nazis with both
ingenuity and evil intent, remained doubtful. Many Jews would
die or be killed, to be sure, but this sort of systematic mass
extermination just did not seem possible in the twentieth century.

Whereas, of course, it is precisely the twentieth century with
its vaunted science and technology that did make it possible.

And what if the world *had* known about Auschwitz while
the gas chambers and crematoria were going full blast? What is
the world doing about ethnic cleansing in Yugoslavia, documented night after night on TV screens all over the globe,
about mass rape and mass murder by a gang of power-mad psychopathic criminals who, unlike the Nazis, could easily be
stopped by a small force at minimal risk?

At any rate, although by 1944 those of us familiar with the
situation in Yugoslavia had well-documented evidence about
the fate of her approximately seventy thousand Jews, most of
them slaughtered domestically, we still knew very little about
the fate of the millions of others who had been deported from
all over Europe and interned in what was referred to as ghettos
and concentration camps. Not until the end of the war did we
grasp, or rather, I should say, learn, the truth. Grasp it we never
did.

In the fall, the Allied Control Commission team whose job it
was to tap the phones and read the mail of Bari's citizens
reported a fascist revival. Some of the top fascist leaders were
still in jail, a few minor ones had gone into hiding, but Bari—
and the South in general—had not gone through the sort of violent purges that later convulsed the northern cities in the wake
of the Allied victory. And whatever that victory—liberation, as

we insisted—had done for pimps, prostitutes and black marketeers, it imposed considerable hardship on the general population, most particularly on young males between their late teens
and their early thirties who, with no jobs and no money, strove
to bolster their sagging self-esteem by acts of vandalism and
patriotic brutality.

It did not take a report by the A-Chee-Chee, as the natives
referred to the acronym of the Allied Control Commission, to
sense the mood in the city. Every night packs of young thugs
roamed the streets, defying the ban on fascist songs while hunting down mixed couples—Italian girls and Allied soldiers—who
had strayed off the main drag and found themselves trapped in
some dark alley. They would cut off the girl's hair, rip off her
clothes and beat up the soldier. It was a titillating sport that fed
on its own excitement, and after a while it got so I never went
out in the evening without a gun. I frequently walked girls
home from the club, and their not being Italian probably would
have made no difference or even been noticed in the heat of
the chase. Whereas a gun—even a .38 colt, a toy by today's
standards of firepower—does tend to get attention. Would I
have used it against unarmed civilians? Probably, if I had been
scared enough. But that thought only scared me much later on
in life.

Autumn in the air uncannily reflected the rapid chilling of
relations between the Partisans and the Allies. On the face of it
the most obvious source of tension was the future of Trieste
and the Istrian peninsula, real enough, to be sure, but also
being exploited by Tito as a diversionary maneuver. His true
concern was not the future of Trieste so much as his own
future and that of Yugoslavia, the consolidation of Communist
power and the elimination of all enemies and potential rivals by
the time the war had ground to its inevitable end. A first step,

taken very much against Stalin's advice, was to detach himself from his Western entanglements and reduce his dependence on the Allies so as to be able to resist their pressure to follow up on his earlier commitment to a coalition government. He had no intention of sharing power with anyone.

Quietly word went out from Partisan headquarters to keep official contacts with Allied personnel to the barest minimum and to put a stop to fraternization. Dragitsa, her eyes apologizing with mute eloquence, would no longer discuss anything other than official business, and that only in the presence of other members of her staff. The Jewish Club was now off limits to PLA personnel; old Belgrade friends had to sneak into my apartment at odd hours, always making sure they weren't being followed. Only Jacob remained contemptuously indifferent to the new code of conduct and continued to see me as before. No party hack was going to tell him whom he could pick for a friend, an attitude which soon after the war got him into serious trouble with the regime and eventually led to his flight from the country altogether.

The chill in the air presaged a major shift in the climate, though few would have predicted the ferocity of the winter to come. A lingering despair spread among the thousands of civilian refugees in Bari, most of them Yugoslav Jews who owed their survival to the courage and humanity of Italians from every walk of life. Their rescue is one of the few bright chapters in the history of World War II; that Italy never received proper credit probably surprises few Italians, who since the days of ancient Rome have cultivated a starkly realistic view of human frailty. Initially these fugitives were content just to have escaped with their lives, but as the war inexorably moved into its final phase, they faced decisions about their future, and even the few who wanted to go back home had to come to terms with the fact that there was no home to go back to. The vast majority opted for Palestine, not out of any burning passion for Zion but because they had been made to realize that they were not welcome anywhere else. Palestine, however, was being governed by the British under a mandate from the League of Nations, and the mandatory power had no intention of permitting the mass immigration of Jews into the land. Thus by the fall of '44 Britain had become one more enemy to the outcasts and aliens seeking a refuge, and what further complicated the situation was the ambiguous role of the Jewish Brigade. On the one hand, it was still part of the British Army, on the other its members became increasingly active in preparing the refugees for life in Palestine and in organizing illegal immigration into the country. Sonya came to see me just before her company was transferred up north and declared herself ready to settle in Italy after the war; according to her, the Italians possessed all the good qualities of the Jews and none of the bad ones. It was an understandable illusion. We made a date to meet in Trieste, but I never got there, and I have no idea what became of her.

TWENTY-TWO

People got drunk on New Year's Eve because custom called for it and because it was one way of keeping warm in those clammy, unheated and unheatable buildings; it actually snowed that night in Bari, for the first time in decades. Even I had a few glasses of red wine and spent the first hours of 1945 in a cubicle of a toilet alternately wretching and passing out.

Not everyone reacts to the tyramine in red wine; a lot of people were just plain sick, and with many of them the hangover began long before they had their first drink. But we all woke up the next morning to the sobering fact that the sixth year of the Second World War had begun and that at this point war and peace loomed about equally menacing. The refugees were looking at yet another year of squatting in some requisitioned dump and being fed by the grace of UNNRA. Beats Auschwitz, to be sure, but when there is only a brick wall ahead instead of a future, people tend to catch brain death from butting their heads against it. Nor did the citizens of Bari have much to look forward to. The Allied troops had brought a fleeting moment of prosperity to the town; as they moved on up north, they took their dirty laundry and a lot of other jobs along with them and left behind a whole new mess of corruption, heartbreak, bastard children and petty crime on top of what had been there all along.

Our own joint operation with the Partisans had for some unfathomable reason—probably just bureaucratic inertia—not yet been suspended, even though Tito's forces by then controlled much of Yugoslavia, including Belgrade. Dragitsa and her staff were desperately anxious to pack up and go home, but like the good little soldiers they were, they asked no questions, waited for orders, and in the meantime produced the daily and weekly summaries which were of no conceivable use to anyone, but which I, another good little soldier, dutifully passed on along with the reports of my own staff, equally useless except insofar as they provided jobs—and the much-coveted preferential ration cards—for a dozen refugees. When I went to see Dragitsa in her office to wish her a Happy New Year, I found her bundled up in her greatcoat looking glum; she acknowledged my wishes with a wan smile, but when I said something about our having been forgotten by the higher-ups, she bristled dutifully. "Comrade Tito does not forget his fighters." *Bullshit* is what I wanted to say to her, would have said to her if we still had been able to talk man to woman. But as it was, she already had tears in her eyes, and I did not want to push things any further; she never would have forgiven me for making her cry.

As for the GIs left in town—mostly Air Force, medical and specialized personnel—we all wanted to go home. Not without apprehension; many of us suspected that you really can't go home again, even if you actually had a home to begin with. But the Battle of the Bulge, the Nazi version of a White Christmas, proved that the Germans, though down, were still far from out. Not to mention the Japanese. And so the choice, as it looked to us on that dusky January morning, was between another year in Europe and a trip to the Pacific.

Personally I was in sort of a limbo and seasoned enough by now not to complain about it. The Bari operation had become pointless, if indeed it ever had a point in the first place, but Rome seemed to have forgotten all about me, which suited me just fine. I had no desire to be remembered by Comrade Eisenhower, and even the ghosts of James Joyce and Italo Svevo could not make me warm up to the prospect of a year in Trieste dealing with lunatics on both sides of the contested border. Under the circumstances, it was a great comfort to still have Jacob in town, even though he seemed to be growing more morose by the hour. He was taking care of his rapidly dwindling patient load and liquidating the hospital while waiting with mixed feelings for his orders to go home.

"So much blood, so much sacrifice," he said on one of our last evenings together. "Was it worth it? They died by the thousands, the best of them, for freedom, equality, a better country, a better world. And maybe they'll turn out to have been the lucky ones, the only ones able to keep the faith."

I had no illusions about the Communists and their intentions, yet I did not believe they would succeed in imposing a Stalin-type dictatorship on a people that had fought so long and so hard for its freedom. It was Jacob, the once-ardent Marxist, who saw things differently, from the inside and, as it turned out, far more accurately.

"We're in for a revolution," he said.

"Isn't that what you wanted?"

"What we wanted was all power to the Soviets. What we'll get is all power to the Partisan heroes. And what power will do to the Partisan heroes is not hard to imagine. Just look at what

it already did to Tito. But the real tragedy is something you people with your simpleminded notions of democracy can't begin
to understand."

"Which is?"

"That whether they like it or not, they've got to hold on to
the tiger's tail or be eaten alive. If the Communists turn soft, if
tomorrow they not only proclaim democracy but actually practice it, there will be no Yugoslavia. The Chetniks and the Ustashe
and the Muslims and the Albanians and the Macedonians, not to
mention hundreds of those roving gangs of bandits that we
were up against throughout the war, will be back killing them
and each other."

"In that case, maybe there ought to be no Yugoslavia."

He shrugged. "They'll still find ways of killing each other."

Lately I have often thought of that conversation, held nearly
half a century ago.

On January 22, the day before my birthday, I had a call from
Rome. The colonel informed me that he might find it difficult
to approve a furlough for me once I started on the Trieste
assignment. Therefore, since I had already been abroad nearly
two years, he had put me in for a thirty-day leave in the States.
Did I want to go?

Of course I wanted to go.

Well, there was nothing "of course" about it. A lot of the
men actually turned down a chance to go home. He assumed it
was because they had found a home in the army. Or gotten one
of those "Dear John" letters.

Or themselves shacked up with a Dear Jane, said I. And wondered, an instant too late, if he was one of them, Rome being
especially conducive to casual bigamy. He seemed to think it
funny, which however proved nothing one way or another.

"How much time do I have to get ready?"

"Your replacement will be on his way tomorrow. The orders should be coming through by the end of next week."

I can't say it was a wrenching farewell, but I had a number of close friends, and the magic carpet still seemed far more real than the jet age. Leaving New York after dinner and getting to Belgrade or Tel-Aviv in time for breakfast would have struck us as science fiction; we did not expect to meet again for years to come, if ever.

My replacement turned out to be an RAF lieutenant, very sure of himself in the manner of minor Oxonians but unsure of everything else, which however made little difference since the operation was obviously about to fold altogether. I was still busy trying to find jobs for our civilian employees when the order came through for me to proceed at once to the Transit Depot, which turned out to be a tent city mired in mud on what had been the Bagnoli racetrack on the outskirts of Naples. Throughout a wet and dismal February I left the sopping tent, my home away from home, every morning like a regular commuter, took the suburban train into the city and spent the day more or less aimlessly walking around, driven as much by anxiety as by curiosity. Naples had changed a great deal in the months since I had last seen it. The exuberant anarchy had given way to a grimly businesslike atmosphere, but while both the local politicians and the Allied Control Commission claimed credit for a minor economic miracle, its true architects were in fact the godfathers of the Camorra, the local crime syndicate, who had organized the systematic pillage and diversion to the black market of huge quantities of supplies and materiel passing through the busy Naples harbor. No one ever even ventured a guess as to how many of our own people were involved in those rackets, primitive though they were by today's standards.

We got so used to our various routines—most men spent

their days sleeping, drinking, shooting dice or playing poker, getting off their bunks only for chow—that it came as a shock to be called out one night and told to be ready for boarding the next morning. Our ship had come in.

Less ship than a floating pigsty, it turned out. It had been sent from New York to São Paolo to pick up Brazilian troops and ferry them to Italy in time for them to claim their share in the conquest of Nazi Germany. Their ardor would, however, have been more appreciated could they have been induced to scrub the latrines and refrain from pissing all over the place; the boat stank as if it had been carrying a regiment of horny tomcats rather than horny Brazilians. They apparently went for U.S. Army food in a big way, but it was no fault of theirs if standard operating procedure prevented this filthy bucket of a Flying Dutchman from replenishing the badly depleted supplies; taking back army food specifically shipped to Italy at great expense obviously made no sense. And while the Army was never irrevocably committed to making sense, in this particular instance it had an additional motive for sticking to the rules: how, when and whether we made it back to the States was of no tactical or strategic importance whatsoever. Fresh reserves destined for overseas are handled with care; it matters whether and in what shape they reach their destination. A bunch of beat-up veterans headed for home didn't warrant any effort or expense. A ladle full of hash on toast—shit on shingles—by way of our daily bread, and no escort even through the Straits of Gibraltar. We could smell the German subs waiting for us out in the cold black waters of the Atlantic and held our breath a good part of the way. You don't ever want to die; but getting shot down on the last mission or drowning on the way home seems downright unfair.

It took nearly two weeks, but in the end we made it, each of us anywhere from five to fifteen pounds lighter than when we started out. The ice-cold quart of milk dispensed on the Hoboken dock by wrinkled Red Cross ladies on behalf of a grateful nation, the first milk we had since we left the States, gave everyone a bad case of diarrhea and reminded me of our arrival in Oran. But at least we had indoor plumbing at Fort Dix and didn't have to balance on a pole. We wasted an entire day being fed, outfitted and lectured at by a brace of unctuous commissioned morons who warned us not to use army language around civilians, and after a sleepless night we were finally off on our thirty-day leave. I skipped breakfast and caught the first train to Philadelphia.

I never did get to Trieste until some twenty years later.

The war in Europe ended the day I reported back to Fort Dix. But Japan refused to surrender, and so the Army stockpiled thousands of us at Aberdeen Proving Grounds for shipment to the Pacific. Until three months later the A-bomb over Hiroshima made all of us redundant.

Time to start living.

TWENTY-THREE

It seems all but impossible to write the final chapter in one's life, because it lacks a clearly defined structure as well as the solid reality of a future time perspective. The script is being written by someone else, while you sit there struggling for air and contemplating the nothingness ahead. Which sounds depressing, and probably is. Then again, it takes a theologian or an idiot to find death other than depressing.

The other problem is the utter banality of a process which, for the individual, represents the culmination of life, the terminal moment that closes the loop. Most of mankind's metaphysical efforts have been directed, in one way or another, toward investing death with meaning, and I salute those who succeed. I can even sympathize to some extent with those of the AIDS Church Militant who blame Clinton for their plight, and who glory in their role as martyrs; may their delusions make it easier for them. As for myself, I prefer to accept the inevitable as inevitable.

I had surgery in the fall of 1992. The lobectomy seemed to take care of the problem, and I indeed enjoyed one glorious year during which I finished a novel and wrote these memoirs. Against all the odds Ruth and I managed to celebrate our fiftieth wedding anniversary in Prague, along with all five members of our immediate family. In the fall we visited all our friends and ex-comrades in Israel and went on from there to tour Provence, ending up in Paris, where my Herzl biography had just been published to some acclaim. While there, I developed a suspicious cough which both Ruth and I desperately sought to ignore but about whose significance neither of us had actually much of a doubt. The cancer, a rather rare variety that is often multifocal and invades the alveoli, had returned and spread to both lungs. Since no further surgery was feasible, I had the choice between chemotherapy and nothing.

Not much of a choice, actually, given the fact that chemotherapy is not curative but at best gives the terminal patient a statistical advantage of a few weeks or months (though some exceptional two-year remissions have been reported), at the price of repeated hospitalizations, utter misery and opportunistic infections due to the assault on the immune system. But we are a nation of gung-ho doers who don't like to resign ourselves even to the most inexorable aspects of fate. And so, we do not go gently into that night. It makes doctors feel better and gives patients the illusion of hope.

Personally I wanted to continue living as normal a life as possible under the circumstances, and on the whole I think I succeeded. Where I failed was in judging the time left to me; once the avalanche gathered speed, things quickly reached the crisis point. Hooked up to an oxygen tank, needing full-time attendance, I shall now try briefly to tell the rest of the story as long as brain, breath and gut hold out.

THE
FINAL CHAPTER

by Miriam Pawel

And that was as far as he got, leaving me, as he put it, to briefly fill in the salient details of the rest of "an outwardly uneventful life."

Which sounded a far easier task in those final weeks when he kept saying, "You'll write the last chapter . . ." and I assured him I would, no problem.

But faced with summing up almost fifty years of life in a handful of words imbued with some modest degree of meaning and a fraction of wit sufficient to serve as a suitable epilogue, it suddenly seems daunting indeed.

Particularly if the life in question happens to be your father's.

So I will try to do what he suggested, tell the rest of the story from my point of view—the only one I can have, of course.

My father never wanted to write the last chapter. He wasn't particularly interested in writing about his life after the army and didn't feel he had much to say of urgency or interest. He wrote about Yugoslavia because it was a time and place he had an emotional commitment to, an adolescence that shaped him profoundly, and because he had something to say about the experience of being a refugee. He interspersed his memoirs with ruminations about death and dying as long as the cancer was an omnipresent worry; when he underwent surgery and gained a respite, he stopped writing about his illness. He finished writing the memoirs while still healthy, and deliberately ended where he did, though he knew it needed something more. A last chapter. Maybe two. He said he'd do it when and if he found a publisher.

The day he was to meet with his editor for the first time, my father went into the hospital. Though he firmly believed they would kill him there, he succeeded in thwarting their best efforts and lived three more weeks, two of them at home. He was mentally as agile as ever, and we talked a great deal those last weeks. He told me about saving the hose from the old vacuum cleaner for a time when he couldn't breathe on his own, but finding when the time came to go on oxygen that he wanted to live. And after all, he pointed out, he finished another book during the month he was on oxygen, before the final crisis. We exchanged morbid banter that would have offended the sensibilities of many who didn't know him. He appreciated the opportunity to laugh about death; self-pity was an emotion totally alien to his being right up until the end, and I think it reassured him to know that those he cared about most deeply would carry on in the spirit which, at least in my case, sprang unabashedly from him.

But as for writing itself, he lacked the requisite combination of physical strength and emotional commitment to get further than the two-page postscript he composed on the laptop computer a week before he died, writing around coughing fits, struggling to balance the need for painkillers with the desire to leave the brain unclouded to do what it did so well.

In the final two pages, he made the last statement he cared enough to make—that writing about dying had become so fashionable as to be trite, and that such writings glorify an essentially prosaic process. Though he had thought of keeping a journal about dying, in the end he found it unappealing. "So much drippy drivel has recently been written and published on the subject of death and dying that I may find it hard to articulate genuine and at the same time non-militant feelings about it," he wrote in his last letter, promising his editor to try to write the final chapter nonetheless. "I'll probably find a way of offending just about everyone."

No doubt he would have, if history is any guide. But this time he never got the chance.

Biographers and autobiographers, my father pointed out many times in the years since he became something of an authority on the genre, are notable as much for what they choose to omit as for what they write.

"Autobiography is a peculiar literary hybrid, a blend of fact and fiction that reveals by concealment and conceals by revelation," he wrote in a review. "The gap that separates the life as lived from the life as written poses a challenge to the reader."

And so I'll use that as a rationale for presenting a rather succinct summary of the bulk of his life that he chose not to write about, with the caveat that I'm as much a slave to that dictum as he was and that the following account will be unavoidably shaded by my own choices.

When he was discharged from the army, he returned to New York City, attended the New School on the GI bill ("a complete waste of time"), struggled to find an affordable apartment, struggled to reconcile being a writer with making a living.

My parents ended up in Queens, where my brother was born in January 1946, and where my father had his early misadventures with carpentry and painting and plumbing—some of which he later became quite skilled at, amassing a small workshop in the basement and building much of our furniture.

He was accepted into a graduate program at Yale University just as his first novel was accepted for publication. He happily rejected the prospect of further schooling and temporarily took a job working as a translator for a life insurance company. The temporary job lasted thirty-six years.

"I am a novelist by choice and by commitment; and after publishing my first novel in 1950—a definite critical success that sold about a thousand copies—I discovered that this commitment entailed another one, the matter of making a living while I wrote as I wanted to write. Since I am fluent in six languages, the choice of a trade seemed overdetermined, and for the past twelve years I've been employed as a translator by a major life insurance company in addition to doing some freelance work in publishing," he wrote in 1962 to a motion-picture producer who briefly contemplated a film treatment of one of his novels. "It is an arrangement that from the practical viewpoint has served its purpose quite well."

The Island in Time, a novel about a group of Jews in a displaced persons camp, was widely hailed as a promising first novel and, those being the days when newspapers were still flourishing and printed not only reviews but pictures of book jackets, it was analyzed and recommended in dozens of papers across the country.

It was followed in 1957 by *From the Dark Tower*, a novel about a poet who commutes each day on the Long Island Rail Road from his suburban home to his job at an insurance company, writes poetry at night, admires Kafka, and is thrown into an identity crisis precipitated by his best friend's suicide and culminating in a rebellion against his placid suburban existence. The etiquette and philosophy of book reviewing being one hundred and eighty degrees different from current mores, all parallels between the author's life and his fiction were carefully omitted from the published critiques. Coming on the heels of William Whyte's groundbreaking *Organization Man*, the novel was praised as a thought-provoking and wry probe of the cost of success in the business world—at a time when that world was rapidly expanding and the phrase "gray flannel suit" was becoming a metaphor for success. European reviewers raved about the novel and welcomed it as proof that the materialistic world of America was indeed as destructive as they had suspected.

His third and last published novel appeared in 1960, a story about the world of psychoanalysis with a plot that revolved around a retired analyst who is haunted by a former patient and friend. My father considered *In the Absence of Magic* his best work to date. Reviews were positive, but more reserved; it seemed less popularly accessible and there were inferences it was almost too "intellectual"—an epithet that dogged him even more in the decades to come as the world of publishing changed dramatically and there was little room for risking fiction that might appeal to anything less than the lowest common denominator.

Several years before the third novel appeared and shortly before I was born in 1958, my parents scraped together enough money to buy a house in Great Neck, then a young community already well known for its schools and attracting a growing Jewish middle class.

My father was an odd fit in suburbia, and perhaps nothing surprised me more upon his death than the outpouring of affection from a community in which I, as a child, always regarded him as something of an iconoclastic, acerbic misfit. (Not that those he habitually sparred with would be given to express the type of sentiments that he himself often made upon the passing of some unfortunate soul he deemed the world a better place without.)

I knew, growing up, that he was different, and, for the most part, I reveled in that fact, having acquired at an early age something of his pride in nonconformity. No one else's father rode a bicycle to the train station every morning, risking fines and engaging in 1971 in one of his trademark letter-writing campaigns when told a village ordinance prohibited chaining the bike to the railroad fence because the tires might damage the sidewalk. No one's father commuted each day on the LIRR—and then went downstairs "to work" each night after dinner, retreating to his pipe smoke-filled basement lair to write novels, book reviews, magazine pieces. No one else I knew had a house that regularly filled with various members of what might loosely be termed the New York Jewish intelligentsia. No one else had a family that took them out of school for weeks each year to travel to Europe or Mexico—but didn't own a second car (a financial priority that was the subject of much amazement among my friends' families).

But if my father suffered occasional angst over surviving the Holocaust and the war to do battle against inane officials and crabgrass, for the most part he felt as at home in Great Neck as the refugee in him probably would have felt most anywhere. The institutions that mattered to him won his emotional commitment—the library, the parks, the schools. His frequent diatribes to the editor of the weekly newspaper—on subjects ranging from laser discs at the library to shuttle buses for high school students unwilling to walk two blocks from the parking lot designated for their luxury cars—were infused even at their most acidic with an intelligence and sense of constructive rather than destructive outrage.

Though not destined or designed for mass audiences, his letters were a rich reservoir of literary talent. He was a prodigious and brilliant letter writer—to friends scattered across the globe; to teachers and school officials who offended by their stupidity or arrogance; to editors of publications of all sorts—and his epistles were generally infused with his irrepressible and unique brand of humor.

Some of them even found their way into print. In a letter published in *The New York Times Book Review* in 1966, he responded to a recent review that said: ". . . there is more to California than the mask of the bizarre behind which the state hides."

"I would appreciate," my father wrote with the juvenile glee he never outgrew, "your asking [the author] what makes him think that California is hiding a mask of the bizarre behind. I thought that, on the contrary, they had sent it to Washington for display in the U.S. Senate. . . ."

But while letter writing was an outlet for instant gratification, the bulk of his compositions were of a much longer, more painstakingly polished sort—and often, by necessity, a more private source of satisfaction. He finished several more novels and became a regular contributor to book reviews and magazines. Along the way he wrote a number of pieces on Heinrich Böll, and when Böll won a Nobel Prize in 1972, my father's writing was suddenly noticed by an astute executive at the insurance company who plucked him out of his peaceful existence deep in the bowels of oblivion and plunked him down in the middle of corporatedom, where he found he'd become a public relations executive, writing speeches and corporate reports.

This did not, of course, affect his basic vision of self.

"As to identity, always in crisis," he wrote in a June 1973 response to a query about how he wished to word the blurb at the end of a magazine article. "Ernst Pawel is a novelist and critic. He regularly contributes to a number of Jewish and general publications and is presently at work on a novel."

I once had a professor who said, in illustrating the difficulties nationalism posed for socialists, that his daughter identified herself as a woman, a Jew and a socialist, in that order. It's a line that's stuck with me for some reason, not for its brilliance but its neatness as an organizing principle, and to paraphrase I'd identify Ernst Pawel as a writer, a father, a Jew, and a runner, in that order.

To take them up in reverse, working back to the peculiarly successful coda to his writing career:

Running was only one of a number of athletic passions; he swam, he bicycled, he played tennis for a while, he race-walked when his knees couldn't stand running anymore, and late in life he joined a health club and worked out on rowing machines and stationary bikes, cursing the television babble that was the obligatory accompaniment. Until an asinine doctor told him a month or so before he died that his oxygen level was alarmingly low and he should refrain from any exercise—after all, he might kill himself; the irony of this, which would ordinarily have amused him greatly, was lost at that point in time—he went to the health club every day. Thus mile by mile, machine by machine, he could measure in an almost detached way the precise degree to which the physical health he valued so much was deteriorating each day.

But running was his first love, and he was a fast runner (sub seven-minute miles in routine workouts). "It may be hard now to remember, but twenty years ago the few of us who took up running as a sport were dismissed as far-out freaks," he wrote in a 1985 essay. ". . . But public ridicule merely fuelled our sense of superiority; the illusion of being ahead of one's time fosters precisely the sort of haughty spirit that goeth before the fall—just before, that is, a pothole, wet garbage or a patch of ice sent you limping off to the medicine man for treatment of whatever you cracked, pulled or tore. With luck, that's what you got.

What you neither got nor expected was sympathy. . . . There is a price to be paid for being out of synch with the rest of the world."

Eventually, the rest of the world caught up with him, and the athletic exploits that once branded him an alien on the streets of Great Neck later earned him trophies in the local races that sprang up as *everyone* began to run.

Quite the reverse was true about his place in a constellation that mattered to him far more—Judaism. There, he became more out of synch as time went by.

Always a secular Jew, he despised the ultrareligious, dismissed reform Judaism as essentially a convenient cop-out, was often critical of many Jewish organizations and became in the last two decades increasingly alienated from and disenchanted with a culture that once was a common and reassuring thread interwoven through the various worlds he inhabited.

His personal angst over the *embourgeoisement* of the Jewish intellectual became a public controversy with the publication of a 1973 article in which he angrily condemned the alarming rightward turn of the Jewish so-called intellectual community in general and of *Commentary* magazine in particular, viewing the growing conservative shift as an abandonment of traditional American Jewish commitments to social justice and responsibility. It was a product, he argued, of an increasing blurring of values between what was Jewish and what was simply middle-class, though he was not completely pessimistic about the long-term prognosis: "This stance of smugness does not yet come naturally to a Jew. For among the least definable but most prominent and durable traits that go with being Jewish is a healthy sceptisicm born out of the exacerbated awareness of the past—an attitude which makes it hard to forget that 'making it' is neither a moral victory nor a very permanent state of affairs but at best an obligation of sorts."

From the characters in the fictional camp for displaced persons of his first novel to the sketch of Heinrich Heine in his final book written more than four decades later, he explored over and over again in his writing the worlds of Jews and what it meant to be Jewish. In the intervening years came magazine articles on everything from the impact on Great Neck schools of the declining support of the Jewish middle class to reflections on modern kibbutzim, a book on the founder of Zionism and a fictional account of the scribe who witnessed the fall of Jersusalem.

The strength of his Jewish identity stemmed from the era in which he came of age; hence it could scarcely be transmitted intact to the next generation. Not so his passion for running, clearly a genetic trait passed on to both his children as a compulsion, as much mental as physical, to be in motion.

That was only a small part of his paternal influence. Ahead of his time there too, he was half of a two-parent working family long before latchkey kids were the subject of popular study, and he was an active and involved father. Back in Queens, he picked my brother up from elementary school one night a week, and while my mother was out working he cooked dinner—baked beans and chocolate pudding. Every week. Though he never did learn to so much as make scrambled eggs, he participated fully in other household chores, and whether a product of his early socialist and Zionist experiences or simply his personality, he was extraordinarily committed to his family and all the work that entailed.

It was only well into my adult years that I realized, not with surprise but with that odd sense of recognition that comes from having something you took for granted admired as unusual, that many of my friends viewed my parents and their close relationship as role models. My father, of course, was typically understated about his home life, and his marriage of fifty-one years. "It was unusual in the sense that we had a good family," he said toward the end. "No marital problems. No children on drugs. That's unusual enough among the general population, let alone among writers."

But then, this is perhaps the area where I'm on shakiest ground, lacking even the pretense of any objectivity or distance; so suffice it to say he invested great time and energy in being a husband and a father, and from my point of view succeeded.

Above all, of course, he defined himself as a writer. He wrote because he had to, and while he wanted his work published and read, that was secondary. He lived by a strict set of inner principles that even if I wished to I could at best only haphazardly reconstruct, and it would seem a pointless and intrusive exercise. The bottom line, to use a term crucial to the industry that he had such difficulty making peace with, is that no book by Ernst Pawel was published for twenty-four years.

I would say that there is nothing like decades wandering in the desert to make the promised land look good, but I know he didn't really believe in the promised land; he subscribed to Kafka's observation that Moses didn't reach the promised land not because he didn't live long enough but because he was human.

Still, when finding oneself suddenly catapulted into the world of literary lions at the age when most people are retiring, it is a most human response to be happy, even if the happiness is tinged at all times with the knowledge that such recognition is often fleeting and fickle indeed.

The Nightmare of Reason, a biography of Franz Kafka, was published in 1984, four years after my father began research and two years after he took early retirement from the insurance company to write full-time. The biography quickly took its place as the definitive work on the Prague Jew whose prescient fiction has had such a powerful effect on generations. It won awards. It was translated into eleven languages. Its author became a speaker in demand at conferences around the country and in Europe. Accustomed to viewing dress-up clothes as the jogging suits with designer emblems instead of the sweats with holes, he had to rent a tuxedo for the first time in his life. And a second and third time.

The immediate impetus for the book was a trip to Prague in 1978, but the idea had taken root long before, back in the early chapters of this book.

"Writing biography has a great deal in common with marriage," he wrote in an essay. "It is a partnership between subject and biographer, in which the partners choose each other for all the right or wrong reasons—usually a mixture of both—ranging from love to hate and from greed to glory. . . . In my own case, the choice of Kafka seemed almost overdetermined. To begin with, he was the great discovery of my adolescence. I am sure I did not do him justice at fifteen. But the life of a stateless Jewish refugee in prewar Europe was nothing if not Kafkaesque, and his stories spoke to me in a way that made the Werfels, the Wassermanns and Schnitzlers of that generation seem tepid and trivial. (Which still strikes me as a sound opinion, one of the few I've had no reason to change.)"

Not surprising then that after Kafka his next choice was Theodor Herzl, the founder of Zionism and in some sense the father of the modern state of Israel. Not bogged down by the necessity of commuting to a job each day, he completed that biography much faster, and it was published to critical acclaim in 1989. It was almost as well received as the Kafka book, and though its intrinsic appeal was to a far more limited audience, it was an audience that mattered much to my father. The book was also a vehicle that allowed him to travel extensively, during its preparation to Israel, a country he had strong if not unambivalent feelings about, and later to France where the book did especially well.

The Labyrinth of Exile cemented his reputation as a talented biographer who wove the historical, social and political contexts seamlessly into the framework of his subjects' lives, telling the story not only of the person but of the time and place as well. One of the few literary regrets I heard my father express was that no one had pointed him in the direction of biography sooner, since it was a genre he both enjoyed immensely and that showcased his talents so well.

After Herzl, he abandoned biography for a bit, writing a fictionalized account of the life of the scribe Josephus. And then, when he was first diagnosed with lung cancer, he began writing his memoirs.

Shortly after the cancer recurred, he signed a contract for a project he had embarked on earlier, a sketch of the last years of Heinrich Heine. The celebrated German poet literally was dying for eight years, suffering from a slow and extraordinarily painful disease that was never accurately diagnosed and essentially confined him to his room from 1848 till his death in 1856, where he did some of his greatest work. The book chronicles the dignity of his dying, the brilliance of his writing and its triumph over his illness, and the turbulent times he could observe only from his "mattress tomb."

It was a book my father always wanted to write, but there's no question that the timing was propitious; it kept him going and gave him a reason to live and, in some very obvious sense, served as an inspiration.

He finished it the day before he went into the hospital, and he died three weeks later.

My father wrote a lot about the importance of humanity. The characters in his novels struggle to be human and wrestle with the forces that conspire to wrest that humanity away. "To be human, to be ourselves is in this day and age an act of revolutionary implications," says the protagonist in *From the Dark Tower*. Asked by the editor of an anthology to select his favorite passage from *The Nightmare of Reason*, my father picked this:

The world that Kafka was "condemned to see with such blinding clarity that he found it unbearable" is our own post-Auschwitz universe, on the brink of extinction. His work is subversive not because he found the truth, but because, being human and therefore having failed to find it, he refused to settle for half-truths and compromise solutions. In visions wrested from his innermost self, and in language of crystalline purity, he gave shape to the anguish of being human.

My father's own humanity resonated in everything he did. Which explains the enormous outpouring of warmth and memories after he died from people whose lives he had touched in myriad small and great ways, from casual conversations on the track to lifelong friendships. He strove beyond anything else to maintain his humanity, often against great odds, and often I think at great personal cost. I hope above all I inherited that.

New York City, September 1994